Lee Bailey's
COUNTRY WEEKENDS

Lee Bailey's
COUNTRY WEEKENDS

Recipes for Good Food and Easy Living

By Lee Bailey

photographs by Joshua Greene

Clarkson N. Potter, Inc./Publishers

DISTRIBUTED BY CROWN PUBLISHERS, INC. NEW YORK

Designed by Rochelle Udell and Douglas Turshen

Published by Clarkson N. Potter, Inc., One Park Avenue,
New York, New York 10016, and simultaneously in
Canada by General Publishing Company Limited

Manufactured in Japan

Library of Congress Cataloging in Publication Data
Bailey, Lee.
   Lee Bailey's Country weekends.

   Includes index.
   1. Cookery.   2. Entertaining.   I. Title.
TX715.B1564   1983   641.5   82-19952
ISBN 0-517-54880-1

10 9 8 7 6 5 4 3

To my father, who was a marvelous cook
and a generous man, and my mother,
who never learned to cook at all
but sure had style

Contents

THE WEEKEND DEFINED

MORE LUNCHES

MORE DINNERS

THE LONG WEEKEND

Foreword

by Amy Gross

This book started because I wanted Lee's recipes—and something else. I wanted to know how he could have six or eight people for dinner Friday night; eight or ten on Saturday night; offer his houseguests breakfasts, lunches, and midafternoon treats like tomato sandwiches or blackberry cobbler; and still remain amiable.

I really wanted to know why the prospect of dinner at Lee's sets off such a happy anticipation in me. Some little creature in me smacks her lips and says, "Oh, boy!"

Going to Lee's is like going home . . . when going home is what it's cracked up to be. It's that comfortable and welcoming. The house itself provides a lot of the pleasure. It's out on Long Island, angled for privacy at the end of a wretched little road. The view is of dunes and the ocean, a saltwater inlet, tall marsh grass and beach plum bushes connected to the house by a long branched deck. The garden, depending on the month or the year, will feature hundreds of daffodils or poppies, or irises so gorgeous you can't believe either that they're real or that they will ever die, or old shrub roses that almost break your heart, they're so tender.

The living room, like the deck, is designed to allow people to shift between being together and being alone. When it's a time to be together, like before or after dinner, the seating draws people close around the fireplace. You can sit quite upright in the russet wing chair, settle next to people on the couch, or sprawl on the hassock or floor pillows—even here, you have your choice of how you want to be, what is most comfortable for you.

At most, before dinner, there are peanuts or pistachios to eat, and drinks from the walk-in bar, equipped with a very large ice maker. You are invited to fix your own drink, or another guest asks you what you'd like, and then you might act as host for the next guest. This is not only informality—it's being caught in a neighborly tempo, a family naturalness.

Before dinner, Lee is in and out, moving between living room and kitchen. It seems to me that every time I've gone into the kitchen to say hello and see how he's doing, what he's doing is mixing up a batter for biscuits. This is an unlikely coincidence, but as an image of Lee in the kitchen pre-dinner, it endures, and I find it infinitely reassuring, a living verity. As long as there's someone in the country making biscuits from scratch, American integrity is still on its feet.

When Lee finally calls you in to dinner—it is never before 10:00 P.M.; running a meal like clockwork is not one of his priorities—people arrange themselves around a sixty-inch round white table set in a glass-walled wing off the kitchen. This table taught me that round was the table shape for me—it's the most sociable of shapes and does more than any other to bring people together into a group, the quiet types as comfortable as the major talkers. Conversation, at least at Lee's round table, is never to the left and then the right or whichever way it's supposed to go. Conversation here is less like a minuet than a ring dance. What it's really like, to switch metaphors, is a big stewpot in the middle of the table. The look of the table—to get back to the business at hand—is of utilitarian luxury. Each person must contend with only one fork, knife, spoon, plate, glass, and each of these elements has a handsome functional honesty—each makes sense. And then, to bollix any aura of hard-edge chic, there are large cotton napkins in oxford-shirt pink.

Well, at last we've arrived at the food.

The first impression, always—whether the food is on the round table or lined up as a buffet on the long pine table in the kitchen—is of a splash of color, a profligacy of dishes, abundance, generosity made tangible, edible. There is always an impression of being offered *extras,* special treats over and beyond the obligatory meat/veg/starch. There'll be cut-up, peppered peaches alongside the ham-and-yam potpie, or tomatoes sliced and sandwiched with honey or with thin discs of lemon—this at a time of the year when the marriage of tomatoes and basil is becoming tedious. There'll be those hot biscuits, or wedges of johnnycake, or (wonderful memory) an awe-inspiring coconut cake with its blizzard of fresh coconut flakes—this, during a period in food fashion when everyone else was serving something fey with poached pears and as few calories as possible.

Here, clearly, is one of the reasons for greedily anticipating a dinner at Lee's. Of course the food will taste good—that's a given. But the choice of food will always be surprising . . . it promises new sensations . . . and it will always be mysteriously satisfying.

The surprise element has to do with the fact that Lee always goes his own way. During the first rush of nouvelle cuisine, he entertained one night with the best boiled beef I've ever eaten—a hefty, real-food kind of meal that was a tremendous relief from all the meticulously turned turnips and shredded leeks and morsels of duck then being exhibited on plates. Food as art is quickly wearying. Chicken potpie, during those crudité years, was Lee's choice for a big buffet party; chicken potpie has only recently emerged as a trendy restaurant item. The new hunger for food redolent of Americana—the new appreciation for the down-home, earthy, honest, hearty, regional—is a corrective to the craze for French food that made boeuf bourguignon more familiar to many of us than beef stew. It has to do with an appetite for basics; a desire to touch base with one's own heritage; to shake off, perhaps, the constraints of European overrefinements; a reevaluation of native products and esthetics.

Lee, clearly, was there—here—first, because he kept following his own inclinations, directed by the same style that has made Bailey/Huebner, and now Lee Bailey at Henri Bendel, the design source it is. It's a consistent style, whether it is applied to food, the shape of a coffee cup, the layout of a room, or friendship. The attitude always makes sense, praises reason and logic. It arises out of a desire to please rather than impress, a sense of economy that wants to see a thing be what it most simply is, and an individuality that is guided by following one's own palate, tastes, and pleasures—a route that requires some courage but by definition has its own rewards. To make your

food interesting, he indicates repeatedly, serve what you really like the way you really like it. (The subtitle of this book, maybe, should be *How to Be Your Own Best Cook*.)

The other thing I like about Lee's way of cooking is that it's easy. It takes into account that one is a home cook and not a restaurateur. I have a lovely collection of cookbooks that can tell me how to spend four days making a three-star restaurant's famous dessert. The only thing is, I no longer have four days to devote to constructing any dessert, nor do I have the nerves to tackle something like a cream sauce that's just itching to curdle. In the recipes here, there is nothing tricky or tetchy. The cooking processes called for are sturdy, resilient, and can take a lot of abuse, approximation, rough measures. Guests who might not volunteer eagerly to reduce a sauce to a glaze can easily get into this act.

And the menus themselves, you will notice, make less work for everybody. The basic two-course structure means that there's a minimum of your jumping up to clear dishes and guests tormentedly worrying whether to be helpful in the kitchen or social at the table. Of course, you can break the meals down to any number of courses, add a first course if you like first courses—I sometimes do, and for some meals like to have salad separately—but Lee's way is an idea about simplifying.

Have I solved the mystery of why Lee's food is so satisfying? The clues are here—from the comfort one feels to the sense of being *given* and indulged . . . to the fact that his pleasure in cooking comes through. I think "pleasure" is the important word, and "pleasing." This is a book about feeding friends, the people who please you. It's about a style of home entertaining that has everything to do with having a good time and almost nothing to do with necessity, obligations, rules. It has to do especially with ease, with unpretentiousness, generosity, surprise, freedom, finesse without chichi. It's about meals that make a direct and unabashed appeal to the taste buds, nose, eyes, with an aim to delight.

It's a book, after all, about country eating, and takes advantage of the freshness of country food, and adheres to the country rule of eating true to season . . . and—since seasonal foods are so good and pass so quickly—eating with gusto.

Introduction

Colette once remarked that she always wanted to see her rooms crowded with flowers and her kitchen table set with whatever seasonal delights the farmers' stalls had to offer: baskets of spotted quail eggs, yellow, noisy-skinned onions, tied bunches of perfect leeks, succulent red berries. She wanted to smell the reassuring odors of good food cooking. And she always wanted her windows, their sills filled with pots of herbs and sweet geranium, to open out into the embrace of tree branches. These things, she said, gave her a sense of peacefulness. It was only in her middle years that she came to fully understand what she had always half known—that wherever she lived she was trying to re-create the country atmosphere of her childhood.

Throughout my life, I realize, I have felt the same yearnings and have depended on some of the same rituals and requirements to make myself at home, both literally and figuratively. This, in spite of the fact that I have lived most of my adult life in a city. I remember how anxious I was years ago to put aside my bumpkin self in favor of what I thought of as a snappier model. Understanding this foolishness amuses me now. I guess I will always be a country person no matter where I might live.

My native South, which indelibly marked me for perpetual country-boyhood, was, and is, home to many for whom entertaining is a way of life. When this tradition first took hold several centuries ago, the South was mostly rural, and guests were probably hard to come by—so people naturally wanted to do their best. Unlike the great urban areas of the East, which held out the possibility of more sophisticated and diverse social events, the South depended on homemade pleasures. With narrowed options and surroundings of bucolic abundance, dining naturally became the centerpiece of most Southern entertainments.

From what I've been told, in those days a typical year was characterized by an endless series of picnics, racing days, church socials and meetings, birthdays, and anniversary celebrations—at which great quantities of simple and delicious food were served. Even deaths were marked and noted in a similar manner. The principal sports then were hunting and fishing, as, in many parts of the South, they still are today. These favored pursuits provided the excuse (and the raw material) for more feasts. Since this also was the heyday of the house party and the extended visit—sometimes lasting months, between even the most distant of relatives—these notions of hospitality got such a good workout that they slipped permanently into the fabric of the culture. Most likely it was the customs of this place during that long-gone moment that transformed "just living well" and comfortably into the peculiarly American brand of gracious living that many of us still find seductive today.

This society passed its attitudes and conventions on down through the generations in the way of such things, and so they came to me through my family, especially my father, a wonderful cook who loved to entertain relatives and friends. He did it all in the spirit of fun and conviviality—making it seem off-handed was part of the game. My father's influence holds me even today. I can feel it when I'm asked as often happens, why entertaining is so easy for me. At those times I'm forced to confess that it isn't as it may seem. The truth is, although I enjoy entertaining and feeding friends, it isn't no work at all, which would be impossible. Like my father, I just want an *illusion* of effortlessness. There is a kind of appealing grace in having the end result of a project, food or otherwise, seemingly brought off without strain. This slightly bogus ease also creates an inviting atmosphere for guests, thereby letting anyone off the hook who might want to lie around all day reading or frying in the sun. They don't have to feel guilty, which is as it should be. After all, weekends are more than cooking and clearing. Some people do their part by entertaining other houseguests or telling you stories or just

appreciating the garden. Frankly, as a guest, my idea of a good weekend is one in which not too much is expected of me. As a host, I try to keep this in mind, which means people should sleep as late as they like, eat as much as they want to, whenever they want to, and just generally indulge themselves. My job is to provide pleasant surroundings and food and drink. Because this produces a sort of free-flowing atmosphere, I usually never invite extra people over for lunch (unless they happen to be around when my houseguests are ready to eat) or accept those luncheon invitations that would cause everyone to stop what they are doing (nothing?), get dressed, and go off someplace at an appointed hour.

And in the evening, if the house is invited for drinks, I don't feel it is the duty of my people to follow along after me if they would rather stay home, and I want to go. I just make it clear that they have a choice.

Dinner guests are asked to come rather late, to give everyone time for a nap and one last walk on the beach. Interestingly enough, mealtimes tend to be very lively. I know a lot of good talkers, but I don't necessarily think that is the reason. More likely it is just a reaction to the quiet mood of the day. Whatever the reason, conversation is seldom boring.

For those who like it to be, the weekend can be a group effort. Many people genuinely enjoy doing a few chores. You can almost always spot a sincere offer, so when I feel one is, I accept. Shelling peas, shucking corn, snapping beans, gathering pinecones for kindling, bringing in firewood, setting the table, picking flowers, going to the village for papers or for something you might have forgotten, or even taking the garbage out—in short, any of a myriad things that anyone can do—if handed over to someone else can make a difference. Seize the chance when a guest offers to do those things that you find tedious, as mixing drinks is for me. (If I get no offers, I encourage guests to make their own, giving me one less thing to concern myself with.)

Not to belabor the point, but the truth is that most people like to participate as long as it is on their own terms. It's not necessary that they use a carbon copy of your own methods to be helpful, either. For instance, I have a friend who loves to arrange flowers and do table settings. Her taste in these things runs slightly counter to mine, but when she comes for a visit I gladly turn it all over to her. Often the results are a pleasing surprise (for us all), and at the same time a couple of household tasks are taken care of.

So the weekend requires work, pleasant work maybe, but work nonetheless. Perhaps if I tell you how I do it you might find something there to uncomplicate your own planning.

I'm a list maker. I even go so far as to map out where I'll have to go to buy certain things and the route I'll take. Except for buying plants and fresh produce, I don't care much for shopping, so I try to get it all over in one trip. Also, I prefer doing everything in the mornings, leaving the balance of the day clear.

I discovered long ago that I enjoy fiddling with several things at one time. While a pot simmers on the stove I'll go to work in the garden for a few minutes, or maybe I'll sit in the sun to talk with a friend while shucking corn. Then I'll stop and read the paper. All this stopping and starting seems to keep chores from becoming tiresome.

I have a fairly uncomplicated approach to flower arranging: big branches or a mass of common garden flowers arranged in a large container are my favorites. When really pressed for time I find a few perfect blooms from the season's first bounty arranged in individual containers will do equally well. I like either extreme.

As for table decorating (although the term puts me off, as the word "brunch" does), it is hard to beat a simple, large plate whose design and color don't compete with the food, a simple glass that makes the wine seem to float in air, a great big soft napkin of any color that strikes your fancy, and pots of field flowers (or weeds) or a few poppies. Although, of course, it is not always so, experience tells me that when there is an awful lot going on on the table besides the food, there hasn't been enough going on (or the wrong thing) in the kitchen. Since we are considering country dining here anyway, fancy table dressings seem a bit "suburban" to me. What is important is balance and appropriateness.

I have the liquor and mixers delivered. Over the years whenever I've been cornered about a house gift I've settled on wine, so now it usually arrives with the guests or is already on hand from a previous guest's stay. A few cases bought in the spring serve as a backup. Being partial to red wine makes choosing even easier for me than for most.

Since I don't like to be stuck in the kitchen all evening, I've always been attracted to recipes and menus that can be prepared at least partially in advance. Complicated or temperamental dishes are saved for another day. My menu planning is further simplified by the fact that they almost invariably are built around one particular item. Generally, those of us who are interested in food have recipes in the backs of our minds we want to try. At different seasons favorite vegetables and fruits appear in the market, and these can provide inspiration too. A simple cookie, a grand meat dish never before tried, or a special treat for a guest, once decided upon, defines your menu choices and makes the process easier by reducing options.

As an example, I might want to prepare a dish using the small hybrid eggplants that turn up in the summer. Since they have a subtle flavor and distinctive texture, a meat served with the dish should be a complement or the eggplant itself will have to be highly seasoned. (Of course, if you and your friends are especially fond of eggplant, you'd likely choose something that would recede to leave the eggplant in all its subtle glory . . . but this is risky unless you know your guests' tastes fairly well.)

To further help, there are combinations of vegetables that are traditional, even inevitable, being repeated in every country where they thrive together. One of the eggplant's natural partners is the tomato. Its sweet, acidic flavor marries well with the texture and taste of eggplant. My point is that one decision leads to another, aided by some automatic choices.

Rice, grits, and other grains or starches such as potatoes and pasta are regulars. I think of these as highly flexible balances and connectors, which can be as simple as a boiled potato or as special as a pasta soufflé. So here you have another decision simplified.

Green salads, on the other hand, are not automatically included with every meal. I don't like them before the main course, and I don't often bother with them after because by then people seem not to be too interested. When I do serve a salad, it is generally chopped to be eaten along with the rest of the course. Chopping makes it easier to cope with and somehow seems to make it more acceptable as a vegetable. The exception is tomatoes, which I suppose are considered salad. They are served in various forms with meals all during their season. I like them especially to balance menus with a pronounced starch content.

When certain favored vegetables, like corn or asparagus, are in season, I usually cook them the pure and simple way only once or twice at the beginning of the season. Then I either avoid them for a while, to prevent monotony, or prepare them in a slightly different manner and combine them with other vegetables. For example, when you have had about all the steamed corn you can stand, try cutting it off the cob and mixing it with zucchini and tomatoes and a few onions. When asparagus gets to you, it can be transformed by preparing it in the Chinese manner—cut diagonally into small pieces and sautéed in peanut oil with a drop of sesame oil, covered briefly to finish, then sprinkled with toasted sesame seeds.

As for meat, I tend to stick to chicken and veal, prepared in the simplest way, with boiled beef, or barbecued lamb, or fish for a change. The vegetables and surprising combinations and extras surrounding the meat or fish component are what really give a meal its personality, as far as I'm concerned.

I like breads and biscuits, so they often appear at my table. They aren't necessary, but if you have the time, why not? Corn bread certainly tastes right with fresh vegetables, and from a practical point of view, both biscuits and corn bread are quite easy to start in advance. All the dry ingredients, along with the butter in the case of the biscuits, can be combined and left to rest in the refrigerator (for biscuits) until half an hour before dining.

I do make desserts, because people expect them, although I suspect they are more tempted by the idea than the reality. Personally, I prefer them served at odd times, like midafternoon, with tea or milk.

I want to be clear that this is how I like to plan meals for my guests. You don't, of course, have to follow my example exactly. Your own unique way of doing things, if it works for you, is just fine.

Except for some with mixed ancestry and a few Oriental and Italian arabesques, these menus are put together out of recipes filled with the flavors I knew while growing up in Louisiana. Many of them originated in the kitchens of the area long before I was born. That, generations later, they have found their way into a book about the simple joy of country eating seems to me fitting indeed. The doing of this made me focus on a time of my life, common to us all, when the knottiest problems yielded to a dish of just-cranked vanilla ice cream or a sugar cookie. It made me realize, once again, how powerfully evocative and satisfying the foods of our childhood that spring from family tradition can be for us all.

—LEE BAILEY
Bridgehampton, New York
Summer 1982

Lee Bailey's
COUNTRY WEEKENDS

THE WEEKEND

The "no-work" breakfast.

DEFINED

The Weekend Defined

Friday

Friday is usually when both you and your guests arrive, and if you don't bring them along with you, there is an even chance one of them will come late. The more guests, the more likely a slow-down, so be ready. Don't make a rigid schedule.

If you plan to make dinner that evening, and want to enjoy doing it, you almost have to go out early, which is what I try to do. It is also important to choose a menu for which the shopping will be easy and which can wait for your guests to trickle in. As a matter of fact, if you can shop for your Friday meal in town before leaving and still miss the traffic, so much the better.

Since it is likely that guests will be tired and frazzled by traffic or "their week," or both, I give anyone who comes early a little reward food to compensate for their woes. Incidentally, this also helps keep them from hating you too much for already being there all bathed and (seemingly) relaxed. My favorite such reward is the tomato sandwich, made with fresh mayonnaise on dark toasted protein or white bread. In our family this sandwich, using vine-ripened tomatoes, was the equivalent of chicken soup. For a sweet tooth, spicy cake (made the week before—or bought) with a cup of tea does the trick. Let everyone wind down a little before you suggest dinner, no matter how late it might be.

If the thought of a real meal on Friday night is too much for you, make a pasta dish. Everyone loves it, and it is about as easy to do as anything I know. Pick up a box of fusilli (pasta coils) or small shells and prepare the wonderful, simple tomato sauce you will find served with the "Saturday Buffet Dinner" on page 36. If you see them, buy a few hot and/or sweet Italian sausages and cook separately. Slice in rings and pass around to be put on top of the pasta, along with grated Parmesan cheese. Serve a salad, and buy ice cream and cookies or a pie at the local farm stand for dessert. If this is still too much, make a late reservation at the local watering spot and take your guests out. (If *this* seems too much, sell the house and become a guest.)

Saturday

Saturday I start the day with my "no-work breakfast," which is simply an assortment of melons and juice, rolls or brioche accompanied by sweet butter, and different kinds of jellies or jams. And, of course, coffee and tea. I just put it all out and go about my business. I have found that if people want an egg, they are happy to cook it themselves—and when they do want one, they usually are particular about how it is prepared. The night before, I set up the coffee and put out the tea things in case there is a very early riser in the house.

When it comes to lunches, too, I try to make it as easy as I can for myself. For instance, should I be planning to entertain extra guests, if possible I simply expand one of my no-work lunches (which you will come across later). If I want to do something special, I try to make it when we will be going out to dinner; that way I won't have to prepare two large meals in one day. If it doesn't work out like that and I am left with a big lunch to prepare, the dinner that evening will be a modest affair—roast chicken and fresh buttered pasta, a few tomatoes or a chopped salad, with bought ice cream and cookies to finish.

Sunday

Sunday is in many ways the trickiest of all to plan for, because leaving times are often up in the air until the day before and can be changed by the weather or missed schedules. My attitude is, be prepared for anything. But I do have a formula that works for me.

If guests are leaving before lunch or want to be gone by one in the afternoon, I will do a big meal that will be both breakfast and lunch. It is usually served around eleven. This is about the only time I plan anything special for "breakfast-type" meals.

When guests are leaving in mid-afternoon, I'll set out my "no-work breakfast." I follow this simple meal with a light lunch at one.

If it is to be an after-supper departure, then both lunch and dinner will be modest, with dinner served early.

Friday
Dinner

Start the weekend right by finding the best place around your house to watch the sun go down and have Friday evening drinks there—dinner, too, if you can. The open porch of this Victorian house is an ideal setting.

Left: *The Friday meal of veal grillards, steamed cabbage, carrot custard, buttered grits, and beaten biscuits.*

23

Friday Dinner

MENU
(for 6)

Grillards
Grits with Butter
Steamed Cabbage
Carrot Custard
Beaten Biscuits
Key Lime Pie
Wine
Coffee

This menu holds very well. The veal can be put on as soon as you arrive (and have had your own reward food) and just left to simmer. The carrot custard can be made anytime; it reheats perfectly. The cabbage can be shredded and put into the steamer, where it can cook as the custard warms. The pie, which has an uncooked custard filling, goes into the refrigerator. Measure the water and grits and then let them stand ready. Grits take only 2 or 3 minutes to cook while everything else is finishing. The last thing is the beaten biscuits. Don't make these unless you have a food processor; failing that, make regular ones. If things are getting frantic, don't make them at all.

Grillards

It is interesting that veal was originally used to make this dish because at the time it was an inexpensive meat. True to that spirit, I use inexpensive stewing veal. I have tasted many versions of grillards. Some use other spices and herbs, and some use beef instead of veal. The combination of Tabasco and Worcestershire sauce is traditional in this dish, but after you have given it a try as is, you might want to alter the quantities to suit your taste, or try it with your own favorite combination of herbs.

3	pounds cubed veal
1/2	cup safflower oil (or bacon fat)
1/2	cup flour
1	tablespoon minced garlic
3/4	cup chopped onion
3/4	cup chopped green onion (including tops)
3/4	cup chopped celery
1	cup chopped green pepper
1/2	cup peeled, seeded, and chopped tomatoes (or canned crushed tomatoes)
2	teaspoons salt
1/2	teaspoon black pepper
1/2	teaspoon thyme
2	bay leaves
3/4	cup water
3/4	cup red wine
1/4	teaspoon Tabasco sauce
1 1/2	tablespoons Worcestershire sauce
3	tablespoons chopped parsley

Trim any fat or connecting tissue from meat and pound the pieces to 1/4-inch thickness. Heat 1/4 cup of oil in a heavy Dutch oven and brown meat in small batches. Set aside.

Add remaining oil and the flour to the pot. Stir and scrape from the bottom of the pan with a flat-ended spatula to make a dark brown roux. When it starts to brown, it will do so very quickly, so take care to keep it from burning.

Add garlic and all vegetables except tomatoes and sauté until limp. You may add a bit more oil if necessary. Add tomatoes, salt, pepper, and herbs, and simmer for 5 minutes. Add water and wine. Bring back to a simmer and add meat and Tabasco and Worcestershire sauce. Simmer uncovered approximately 1 hour, stirring occasionally to keep from sticking. Remove bay leaves and stir in parsley.

Flavor improves if the dish is allowed to stand several hours before serving, and it is even better if refrigerated overnight.

Serves 6

Grits with Butter

Grits should be cooked at the end of your dinner preparation time. Let stand in a double boiler over hot (not boiling) water if they finish before you are ready for them.

For those of you who might not know exactly what grits are, let me explain that they are simply hulled corn kernels ground coarsely. Their appeal, aside from their flavor, is their creamy texture. Ironically, unappetizing texture is the reason people give when they tell me they have tried grits but don't like them. Usually their introduction has been by way of being served a lukewarm, dry, and lumpy mixture that had been sitting around too long and was indeed unappetizing.

Grits are packaged in three forms, the difference having to do with the length of time they must be cooked. The first is the old-fashioned variety, which must be cooked about 30 minutes. The flavor is excellent, but the grits have to be watched to keep from sticking and getting lumpy. The second, which I often use, can be prepared in about 5 minutes and is referred to as "quick grits." The last is the instant type, which I would avoid because the flavor is too bland.

1½   cups quick grits
1½   teaspoons salt
6   cups boiling water
     Melted unsalted butter

Stir grits slowly into salted boiling water. Return to a slow boil and reduce heat. Cook 5 minutes, stirring constantly. Top with melted butter when served.

Note: After grits are poured from the cooking pan, immediately fill the pan with cold water. This will keep any grits left in the pot from sticking to it.

Serves 6

Steamed Cabbage

I think this vegetable is not used often enough. Many people think it is too homely. Give it a chance.

4   cups shredded cabbage, tightly packed
¼   cup (½ stick) unsalted butter
1   tablespoon fresh lemon juice
¾   teaspoon salt
     Dash of black pepper

Shred cabbage finely. Discard large inner core. Put in the top of a steamer and steam for 7 minutes. If the cabbage is older, this may take longer. Do not overcook.

Remove to a serving dish and pour over it the butter mixed with lemon juice. You can add the salt and pepper to the butter mixture or toss in separately.

Serves 6

Veal grillards and buttered cabbage.

Beaten biscuits and fresh sweet butter.

Sweet, creamy carrot custard.

Key lime pie with fresh strawberries.

Carrot Custard

This has a surprisingly sweet taste that is very nice with meat. It also reheats remarkably well. To do so, put in a pan over just simmering water for 1/2 hour before serving.

14 ounces carrots, peeled and cut into 1-inch pieces
2 tablespoons (1/4 stick) unsalted butter, at room temperature
2 eggs
1/2 cup milk
3 tablespoons evaporated skim milk
1/2 teaspoon freshly grated nutmeg
1/2 teaspoon salt
Dash of black pepper

Preheat oven to 375 degrees and put rack in the middle position. Butter a 9-inch round cake pan and set aside. Put a kettle of water on to boil.

Boil carrots until very tender, about 30 minutes, and drain. In a food processor with a metal blade, process carrots with the butter for 10 seconds. Add remaining ingredients and process for 30 seconds more, until well puréed. Adjust seasoning if necessary.

Pour mixture into the cake pan and put the pan in a large ovenproof pan. Pour enough boiling water around it to come halfway up the side of the cake pan. Put in the oven and bake for 30 to 35 minutes. Mixture will be firm and set. If using immediately, allow enough time to let it rest for 10 minutes after it has been taken out of the water. Do not remove from the pan if you intend to reheat it later. When ready to serve, loosen edges gently with a knife and invert it onto the serving platter.

Serves 6

Beaten Biscuits

The name of these biscuits comes from their method of preparation. It is quite tedious to do by hand, so I use a food processor. I would not suggest making them if you do not have such a machine. They have an interesting texture that makes them quite different from the others that you will come across later in the book.

3 cups flour
2 teaspoons salt
3/4 cup (1 1/2 sticks) unsalted butter
3/4 cup ice-cold milk

Preheat oven to 350 degrees.

Combine the flour and salt in the container of a food processor. Cut the butter into pieces and put it in with the dry ingredients. Process using the metal blade until the mixture resembles coarse cornmeal. Remove top of machine and sprinkle the milk in. Process until the mixture makes a ball. Continue processing for 2 more minutes. This will shake the machine around a bit because of the volume of the dough.

At the end of the processing time remove the dough, which should be shiny and elastic, to a well-floured surface. Turn to flour both sides. Roll out to 1/4-inch thickness using a floured rolling pin. Smooth flour evenly onto the rolled-out dough and then fold it over on itself. Make sure there is still flour on the surface under the dough. Cut into 1 1/2-inch biscuits and place on an ungreased cookie sheet. Prick the tops with a fork. Bake for 25 minutes, until golden brown.

Note: The reason for folding the dough over on itself before cutting is so that the baked biscuits will come apart easily for buttering.

Leftover biscuits are good cold with a bit of mustard and ham sandwiched in them.

Makes about 2 dozen biscuits

Key Lime Pie

I have tried many versions of this old favorite, and I think I have found the best. Not surprisingly, it is the easiest. This is a small pie, but its richness means you will only serve small portions.

1   pint fresh strawberries, sliced and sprinkled with 1 tablespoon sugar (optional)

Crust
1   cup unbleached flour
     Dash of salt
3/4 cup (1½ sticks) unsalted butter
3   tablespoons ice water

Custard Filling
1/2 cup fresh lime juice
1   14-ounce can sweetened condensed milk
2   egg whites, stiffly beaten

When strawberries are in season, this pie is good served with a few sliced ones over the top of each piece. If you are planning to do this, slice the berries and sprinkle with sugar. Allow to sit uncovered in the refrigerator for an hour so that they will chill and give up some juice.

To make pie crust, put flour, salt, and butter, cut into ½-inch pieces, into a food processor fitted with a metal blade. Process just long enough for mixture to resemble coarse cornmeal. Remove top and sprinkle ice water over mixture. Process just long enough to mix well.

Gather the dough into a ball and press into a circle between two sheets of waxed paper or plastic wrap. Seal and refrigerate for an hour.

When ready to use, preheat oven to 425 degrees. Roll out to ¼-inch thickness and place in an 8-inch pie pan. Trim and crimp the edges and prick the bottom of the pan with the tines of a fork. Bake in the oven for 10 to 12 minutes, or until golden brown. Look in on the crust several times during this brief baking period and prick any bubbles that may have formed in the dough. It is important to do this to keep the bottom of the crust flat. This crust shrinks considerably in the pan so don't be alarmed; however, this makes it quite easy to remove. Allow to cool in the pan and then carefully slide out onto a serving plate.

To make the custard filling, mix the lime juice with the condensed milk and stir until well incorporated. Beat egg whites until stiff and fold into the condensed milk mixture. Pour and scrape into the cooled crust and refrigerate the pie until ready to serve.

Makes one 8-inch pie

Tomato soufflé.

Veal loaf garnished with sage.

Saturday Lunch

If you are fortunate enough to have a deck facing the ocean, it makes the perfect place to entertain intimate or large groups of guests. During the day, always shade the dining table; nobody really likes to sit in the hot summer sun to eat.

Left: *green salad, black olives, cheeses, crisp French bread and sweet butter, and big purple plums.*

31

Saturday Lunch

MENU
(for 6)

Tomato Soufflé

Veal and Red Pepper Loaf

Black Olives in Oil and Herbs

Mild Goat Cheese with Olive Oil, Juniper
Berries, Rosemary, and Chives

Boston Lettuce Salad with
Sherry Vinegar Dressing

French Bread and Sweet Butter

Gratte Paille Cheese

Black Plums

Wine

Iced Tea

The centerpiece of this lunch is the tomato soufflé. The tomato base for it can be prepared in advance, but the first thing you must do is make the veal loaf. This is not difficult but should be done early enough in the day for it to cook and cool. The cheese must be at room temperature, so it should be left out of the refrigerator along with the black olives. Lettuce can be washed and dried and put back in the refrigerator, and the dressing made and left out. About 5 minutes before serving, the French bread can be sprinkled with a bit of water and put into a preheated 350-degree oven to warm.

Tomato Soufflé

I especially like this recipe because it is so simple to prepare. The most important thing to understand here is that the success of this soufflé depends on the flavor of the tomato base. The finished dish can be no better than the base, so make sure it is seasoned to your liking before using it. Add more seasoning if it doesn't seem right, and a bit more tomato paste if the tomato essence is not pronounced enough. The tomato base can be prepared in advance.

Always serve the soufflé as soon as you can get people to the table.

3	pounds ripe tomatoes
1/4	cup (1/2 stick) unsalted butter
1	tablespoon tomato paste
3	tablespoons flour
1	cup milk
4	tablespoons Parmesan cheese
5	egg whites
1/2	teaspoon cream of tartar

Preheat oven to 350 degrees. Prepare a 12-cup (3-quart) soufflé dish by dusting it lightly inside with flour.

Core and chop the tomatoes. Heat 1 tablespoon of butter in a large skillet and add the tomatoes. Cook over low heat for approximately 30 minutes to reduce their water content. Be careful not to let them scorch. Strain and remove seeds and skins. You should have about 2 cups of smooth pulp. Add tomato paste and mix. Set aside.

In the top of a double boiler melt the remaining butter and then add the flour, mixing well. Cook for about 4 minutes, stirring all the while. Add milk and continue to stir (or whisk) to eliminate any lumps. Add tomato mixture and blend well. Add cheese and stir until it melts. Allow to cool for about 30 minutes.

Beat egg whites until stiff. Sprinkle the cream of tartar over the top and beat until incorporated. Fold a quarter of the beaten egg whites into the tomato mixture. Pour this a little at a time over the remaining egg whites and fold in with a rolling motion until the two elements are combined. There may still be a few lumps of egg white but do not overmix.

Pour into the prepared soufflé dish and put in the center of the oven for 30 minutes, or until it has risen and is lightly browned on top.

Serves 6

Veal and Red Pepper Loaf

The flavor of this dish improves if allowed to sit a few hours after it is cooked. Before serving I press a big sprig of sage flat on the top for decoration.

2	medium sweet red peppers
1	tablespoon safflower oil
1	cup finely chopped onion
1	small clove garlic, minced
1	cup finely chopped celery
½	pound thinly sliced mushrooms
1½	pounds veal, coarsely ground
½	cup chopped parsley
½	cup fresh soft bread crumbs
1	teaspoon salt
½	teaspoon pepper, or to taste
	Few grinds of nutmeg
1	egg, lightly beaten

Preheat oven to 375 degrees. Put kettle of water on to boil.

Place the whole peppers in a pan under the broiler. Turn them until they are completely blackened, then put them in a brown paper bag and fold the top shut. This will trap the moisture as they cool, making it easier to peel the peppers later. Set aside.

Heat the oil and add the onion, garlic, and celery, sautéing until wilted. Do not burn. Add the mushrooms and cook until their water has mostly evaporated. Add the veal, mix, and turn off the heat. Peel and seed the peppers, discarding the tops. Cut into small cubes. Mix in with the veal. Add and mix in the parsley and bread crumbs. Add salt, pepper, and nutmeg. Add the egg.

Pour and scrape into a 4 × 5-inch ceramic pâté loaf pan. Smooth the top. Set the pan into a larger baking dish and surround with boiling water about an inch up the side of the pan. Bake for 1¼ hours. Remove from the oven and allow to cool in the pan for 30 minutes. Run a knife around the edge to loosen, and invert onto the serving platter. Be careful, as there will be liquid in the pan. The loaf may be left like this until time to serve.

Serves 6

Olives, Cheeses, and Plums

Buy loose, not pitted, black olives in brine, drain and wash, then drain once more. Put them in a bowl. Add enough good olive oil to just cover. Sprinkle with fines herbes or a favorite combination of dried herbs and mix. Allow to sit.

Place a thick round of mild goat cheese on a plate and pour over it a liberal amount of good olive oil. Since this oil will be tasted undiluted, be sure that it is of high quality, same as with that used with olives. Add 6 to 8 juniper berries and roll them around in the oil so that they are well coated. Snip fresh rosemary and chives over the cheese and give a generous grind of black pepper to finish. Serve this cheese and the olives with the soufflé.

If you like plums and they are large, buy 1½ plums per guest. If they are small, buy 2 for each. Serve the Gratte Paille cheese as is at room temperature with the plums.

Boston Lettuce Salad with Sherry Vinegar Dressing

Boston lettuce is one of my favorites. I like it here with no other ingredients and a simple dressing. The hint of sherry blends well with the Tomato Soufflé, which has a very subtle flavor itself.

2	heads Boston lettuce, washed, dried, and torn into bite-size pieces

Sherry Vinegar Dressing

2	tablespoons sherry vinegar
½	teaspoon salt, or to taste
	Few grinds of black pepper
2	tablespoons mild olive oil
3	tablespoons safflower oil

Put lettuce into the bowl in which it is going to be served, cover, and refrigerate until needed.

To make dressing, combine vinegar with salt and pepper and mix. Whisk in the oils. Adjust the seasonings if necessary. When it is time to toss the salad, add about 4 tablespoons of dressing and mix. All leaves should be coated but none of the dressing should collect in the bottom of the salad bowl. Taste and add more dressing or salt.

Makes ½ cup dressing

Early evening light makes this striking house an even more glamorous place for a big outdoor party.

Saturday Buffet Dinner

MENU
(for 12)

Pasta with Two Sauces
Fried Eggplant Sticks
Mushroom and Walnut Salad
Tea Cakes
Iced Coffee Brandy
Wine

Left: *pasta mixed with brown sauce, tomato sauce for topping, mushroom and walnut salad, and fried eggplant sticks.* Below: *spicy iced coffee laced with brandy and served with old-fashioned tea cakes.*

This pasta dinner is easy to expand and organize for a large group. Both pasta sauces can be made a day in advance. The pasta itself is cooked just before serving, and your main course is ready. Remember, it can take a few minutes for the water in which you cook the pasta to come to a boil, so plan for it. The mushrooms can be washed and sliced and tossed with the lemon juice. The other salad ingredients can be prepared and put in to refrigerate. Make the salad dressing and let stand at room temperature. The raw eggplant sticks must be salted and allowed to sit for 1 hour before they can be used, so plan accordingly. The iced coffee can be made and refrigerated hours before dinner, and the tea cakes can be made anytime (or plain cookies bought).

Forty-five minutes before you want to serve, start the eggplant sticks and keep them warm. Put water on for the pasta and start heating the sauces. Combine the salad, but do not dress until time to serve. Get the dessert service ready. The fried eggplant can sit in a warm oven for a bit if your timing is off. Fifteen minutes more or less won't be noticed.

35

Pasta with Two Sauces

To assemble this dinner cook 2 pounds of fusilli pasta (shaped like little coils) until tender but not mushy. Drain and mix with the Brown Sauce. Serve the Tomato Sauce on the side. This way the Tomato Sauce, which has a light, fresh flavor, won't be absorbed by the more pungent Brown Sauce. A bit of freshly chopped parsley can be sprinkled over the top of the dressed pasta, if you like.

Brown Sauce
This is one of the many versions of the classic Bolognese sauces. It can be served as suggested here or over rice or any other kind of baked pasta dish.

1	ounce dried mushrooms, preferably porcini
1/4	cup olive oil
1	medium onion, finely chopped
1	carrot, finely chopped
1	stalk of celery, finely chopped
5	sprigs parsley, finely chopped
1	large clove garlic, peeled and finely chopped
1	small strip lemon peel, chopped
1/2	pound ground chuck beef
1/2	cup dry red wine
1	1-pound can Italian plum tomatoes (without basil or paste)
1	tablespoon tomato paste
	Salt and pepper to taste
2	cups hot chicken broth

Cover the mushrooms with lukewarm water and set aside for 30 minutes. Put olive oil in large skillet and sauté the vegetables (except the tomatoes) and lemon peel until golden brown (about 20 minutes). Add the ground chuck and sauté for an additional 15 minutes. Add the wine and cook until it evaporates, about 20 minutes. Add the tomatoes and tomato paste, mixing thoroughly, and salt and pepper to taste. Simmer very, very slowly for 25 minutes. Drain the soaked mushrooms. (The soaking liquid can be refrigerated and used later in soup.) Add the

mushrooms to the sauce and continue to simmer very slowly for another 1½ hours, adding the hot chicken broth as more liquid is needed. If you do not have enough liquid to complete the cooking time, add the mushroom water. The finished sauce should not be too liquid but of medium density. You can set it aside at this point. Be careful not to scorch when it is reheated.

Tomato Sauce
This is a light sauce, which should be characterized by a strong tomatoey freshness. It has a very brief cooking period to preserve this quality.

4	tablespoons olive oil
1	very large red Bermuda onion, sliced medium thin
3	pounds ripe plum tomatoes, skinned and seeded
6	large cloves garlic, peeled and finely chopped
	Salt to taste

Put the olive oil in a large skillet and sauté onion until wilted but not brown. Add the tomatoes, garlic, and salt. Simmer gently for 30 minutes, until flavor develops and some water evaporates. Do not overcook.

Note: This tasty sauce freezes very well, so if you find yourself swamped with the usual season's-end abundance of tomatoes you might make a few containers to use in the winter.

Serves 12

Fried Eggplant Sticks

Eggplant is a traditional Italian vegetable. Here it has a crunchy texture and does double duty as both vegetable and bread.

2	large eggplants cut into finger-size sticks
2	eggs
1/2	cup milk
	Cornmeal as necessary
	Safflower oil for deep-frying

Sprinkle the cut eggplant generously with salt and let stand for an hour. When ready to use, drain and pat dry with absorbent towels.

Beat the eggs and milk in a bowl large enough to hold a number of sticks at one time. Pour a quantity of yellow cornmeal onto a sheet of waxed paper.

Put about one inch of oil in a large pan and start it heating. When oil is very hot, dip eggplant in the egg-milk mixture and then roll in cornmeal to coat. You might have 6 or 7 of the sticks ready to go at one time. Fry in the hot oil until golden brown. (Since these sticks are comparatively thin, be very careful not to burn them.)

Makes approximately 3 dozen sticks

Mushroom and Walnut Salad

This is an interesting combination of flavors that is a nice change from the traditional green salad.

½	pound mushrooms, carefully washed, trimmed, and sliced thin
1	tablespoon lemon juice
4	ounces walnuts, chopped
3	heads Boston lettuce, washed and torn into bite-size pieces

Walnut Dressing
2	tablespoons red wine vinegar
½	teaspoon salt, or to taste
	Pepper to taste
3	tablespoons walnut oil
2	tablespoons safflower oil

Wash and slice the mushrooms, toss with lemon juice, and refrigerate. Do not do this more than an hour before you are ready to serve. Chop walnuts coarsely.

Make dressing by whisking together the vinegar, salt, and pepper and then adding the oils. Do not refrigerate. When ready to serve, toss mushrooms, walnuts, and lettuce together, and dress with the dressing. Taste and correct seasoning if necessary.

Makes ½ cup dressing

Tea Cakes

Tea cakes were once very popular but seem to have been crowded out by more exotic progeny. By themselves they are unassuming, but when served with, for instance, strong vanilla ice cream or fruit, they come into their own. These little cakes are a perfect foil for the spicy iced coffee.

½	cup (1 stick) unsalted butter
¾	cup sugar
1	egg
½	teaspoon baking soda
1½	teaspoons white vinegar
2⅓	cups flour
½	teaspoon salt

Preheat oven to 350 degrees. Very lightly grease 2 medium cookie sheets.

Cream butter and sugar together. Add egg and beat well. Dissolve soda in vinegar and mix in. Combine the flour and salt and gradually add. Mix thoroughly to make a stiff batter that can be rolled thin.

Roll dough out on floured surface to ¼-inch thickness. Cut with fancy biscuit cutter and place on cookie sheets. Bake in preheated oven for 12 minutes, or until light gold. Remove to cooling rack.

Note: If you like, sugar can be sprinkled on top of cakes before baking. Their flavor improves if they are made a day or so ahead of time. They keep extremely well in a jar with a tight lid.

Makes approximately 2 dozen cookies

Iced Coffee Brandy

Spiced and spiked iced coffee served in this manner was a favorite of a friend of mine, Margaret Williams, from New Orleans. When accompanied by tea cakes, it becomes dessert, coffee, and after-dinner liqueur all in one—perfect for a party.

6	cups very strong black coffee
	Peel of 1 small orange, cut into ½-inch-wide strips
3	cinnamon sticks
18	whole cloves
3	teaspoons sugar
1½	cups good brandy
	Crushed ice

Pour hot coffee into a large heatproof pitcher. Add the orange peel, cinnamon sticks, cloves, and sugar. Taste and add more sugar if you like. Stir in the brandy, more if it is to your taste—but this is a very potent drink. Cool and refrigerate, covered, until ready to use. Serve in Pilsner glasses over crushed ice.

Serves 12

Pan-broiled quail and scrambled eggs.

Hearty Sunday Breakfast

Buttermilk biscuits and fig conserve.

If your setup includes a little guest house, as below, treat its weekend occupants to the luxury of having breakfast in private at whatever time suits their mood. Equip the house with a small refrigerator, a coffee maker, and an extra cabinet filled with simple breakfast fixings.

Hearty Sunday Breakfast

MENU
(for 6)

Pan-Broiled Quail
Scrambled Eggs
Baked Grits
Drop Buttermilk Biscuits
Fig Conserve
Coffee

The idea for this breakfast is borrowed from a favorite childhood meal. I am a bit ashamed to say that its magnitude was not because we were celebrating a special occasion; this was just a regular breakfast. We always had quail during hunting season in the fall. Treat yourself to it at least once; then, since quail are both rare and expensive, a very small game hen can be substituted.

Start with the grits because they take an hour to bake. When the dish is in the oven, prepare the birds and combine the dry ingredients for the biscuits. Put the birds on to cook. Fifteen minutes before the grits are to be done, put the biscuits in to bake. If you have only one oven, you can turn it up to cook the biscuits along with the grits for their cooking time. Scramble the eggs after everything else is ready. I do them quickly in several batches. The fig conserve would have been made in advance.

Pan-Broiled Quail

Instead of being pan-broiled, quail may be baked in the oven like any other small bird. Allow 1½ birds per person.

- 9 quail
- ¼ cup (½ stick) clarified unsalted butter
- 4 tablespoons safflower oil
  Salt and pepper to taste
  Flour for dusting

Butterfly the quail by splitting along the breastbone and striking with the side of a cleaver to completely flatten.

Use 2 large skillets and heat ½ amount of butter and oil in each. Add more butter and oil if necessary. Salt and pepper the birds and dust each slightly with flour. Brown on both sides, pressing them down as you do, and turning frequently. Then reduce heat, cover loosely, and cook until tender, 12 to 18 minutes depending on the size of the bird. Keep warm until ready to serve.

Serves 6

Baked Grits

This dish should be served from the pan in which it is baked. Cooking grits in milk instead of water gives them a very creamy texture and flavor.

- 4½ cups milk
- 1 cup quick grits (not instant)
- ¼ cup (½ stick) unsalted butter
- 1 teaspoon salt
- 2 eggs

Preheat oven to 350 degrees.

Generously butter a 1½- or 2-quart casserole and set aside. Bring 4 cups milk carefully to a boil. Do not scorch. Add 1 cup quick grits in a steady stream, stirring all the while. Cook 4 minutes, continuing to stir. Remove from heat and add the butter, salt, and remaining ½ cup milk. Mix well. Beat the eggs well and add to the mixture. Mix and pour into the prepared casserole. Bake for 1 hour.

Serves 6

Drop Buttermilk Biscuits

Of all the biscuits in this book, these are the simplest to prepare because they do not require rolling out and cutting before being baked. After the butter has been cut in, they only need a few quick strokes and they are ready to be dropped onto a cookie sheet.

2	cups flour
1	teaspoon salt
2	teaspoons baking powder
1/2	teaspoon baking soda
6	tablespoons (3/4 stick) chilled unsalted butter
1 1/2	cups buttermilk

Preheat oven to 450 degrees.

Sift together into a bowl the flour, salt, baking powder, and baking soda. Add the butter, cut into 6 pieces, and blend with a pastry blender or two knives until butter is the size of peas. Add buttermilk all at once and stir just enough to mix.

Drop by tablespoons onto an ungreased cookie sheet. Bake for 12 to 15 minutes, until golden brown.

Makes 1 1/2 dozen biscuits

Fig Conserve

This recipe comes from my aunt who lives in Natchez, where there are a lot of figs. It is delicious and can be used like any other jam.

1	lemon
1	pint small ripe figs, trimmed
1	cup sugar
1/4	cup chopped pecans

Cut the lemon into sections and remove seeds. Chop coarsely in a food processor or chopper. Put the figs and lemon in a saucepan, add the sugar, and boil until thick. Stir in pecans and cool. This can be poured into sterilized jars and sealed. It may also be kept in the refrigerator, unsealed. They say it will keep for months, but it has never stayed around long enough for me to find out.

Makes approximately 1 1/2 pints

Refrigerator Strawberry Preserve*

This recipe came to mind because it is so good with biscuits. When strawberries are plentiful, I make several batches of this simple preserve and then store the jam in the refrigerator. If you are like I am and find the whole process of canning defeating, this is the perfect solution. This technique also produces a fresher tasting jam. The jam will keep indefinitely in the refrigerator as long as it is tightly covered.

1	pint strawberries
1/2	cup sugar
1/2	teaspoon fresh lemon juice

Wash, hull, and quarter berries. In a small enamel pot alternate layers of berries and sugar. Bring to a boil, stirring from time to time, and then turn heat down. Add lemon juice and simmer for 8 to 10 minutes, stirring often.

With a slotted spoon, remove fruit to a small jar. Continue simmering until juice is reduced by half, and pour over berries. Allow to cool. Cover and keep refrigerated.

Note: This jam is not very sweet, which is the way I like it. You may add more sugar to a later batch if you like it sweeter.

Makes 1 small pint

*Alternate to Fig Conserve recipe

Light Sunday Lunch

A view of the river seen reflected in the windows of this handsome house creates just the right atmosphere for a light Sunday lunch: mint frittata, salad, red peppers and mushrooms, toasted rounds of French bread and, for dessert, fresh blueberries and cream.

Light Sunday Lunch

A version of the egg and vegetable dish in this menu appears in most countries: in France as an *omelette,* in Spain as a *tortilla de huevos,* and in China as *egg fu yung.* This is the Italian one, the *frittata.*

The frittata is wonderfully flexible. It can be made with many different combinations of seasonal vegetables and herbs. You may also vary it by adding meat, such as ham.

Mint Frittata

This combination of potatoes and mint is inspired by the memory of a lunch I had in Tuscany, where mint is very popular. When I first tasted it, it was so familiar that I could not immediately identify it. I think you will like it.

2	medium white potatoes
2	tablespoons safflower oil
8	eggs, lightly beaten
4	tablespoons fresh chopped mint leaves
1/2	teaspoon salt
	Pepper to taste
2	tablespoons clarified unsalted butter

Boil potatoes until medium tender and dice into medium-size chunks. Heat oil in a fairly good-size skillet. Sauté potatoes at moderate high heat until they start to brown, about 4 to 5 minutes.

Preheat broiler at this point. Have ready the eggs, to which mint, salt, and pepper have been added. Add the butter to the skillet containing the potatoes, and when it is bubbly, pour in the egg mixture. Stir slightly until it begins to set. Then put under the preheated broiler for several minutes until it puffs and is just beginning to brown. Serve at once.

Serves 4

MENU
(for 4)

Mint Frittata
Green Salad
Roasted Sweet Red Peppers
Marinated Mushrooms
French Bread and Butter
Blueberries and Cream
Wine
Coffee

Being a traditionalist at heart, I regard Sunday breakfast as a very important meal. Lots of people seem to share my feeling, even those who don't ordinarily care much about it during the week. Maybe it has to do with self-indulgent Sunday ways. Whatever, even if I have started the day with only juice, rolls, and coffee, I still like eggs in some form on Sunday—so here a light breakfast is extended into a light lunch using the traditional breakfast egg as the centerpiece. Maybe for you this meal might include another kind of egg dish or, if you are in a festive mood, a classic cheese soufflé. The point is, serve whatever pleases you, and it will probably suit the others as well. Just make two light meals of it in place of one.

Green Salad

You may use a mixture of several light lettuces in this salad, which marries well with a dressing utilizing a fruit vinegar. Although the flavor of this vinegar is interesting, I use it sparingly because it can become a bit cloying.

- 1   small head Boston lettuce
- 1   small head Bibb lettuce
- 1/2   small head loose-leaf garden lettuce

Fruit Vinaigrette Dressing

- 1/2   teaspoon salt
- 1/2   teaspoon dry mustard
-     Few grinds fresh black pepper
- 1   tablespoon fruit vinegar, raspberry or other
- 1 1/2   tablespoons safflower oil
- 1   tablespoon mild olive oil

Wash lettuces thoroughly and pat dry. Tear into bite-size pieces, being careful not to bruise the leaves.

Whisk together the other ingredients to make the Vinaigrette and dress the lettuce lightly.

Makes 1/2 cup dressing

Roasted Sweet Red Peppers

Roast several whole red peppers in the broiler until they turn black. Allow to cool 10 or 15 minutes in a brown paper bag with the end rolled shut. Peel, seed, and cut into strips, then cover with olive oil, and refrigerate.

Marinated Mushrooms

This recipe will make more mushrooms than you need, but they will keep well and are a good addition to any quick meal.

- 1   pound button mushrooms, washed and trimmed
- 1   teaspoon chopped chives
- 1/4   teaspoon chopped rosemary

Dressing/Marinade

- 2   tablespoons wine vinegar
- 2   tablespoons safflower oil
- 3   tablespoons olive oil
- 1   generous teaspoon Dijon mustard
- 1   teaspoon salt, or to taste
-     Few grinds of black pepper

Put the mushrooms in a crockery bowl. Whisk together all the ingredients for the dressing/marinade. Sprinkle the chives and rosemary over the mushrooms and toss with the dressing. Marinate for at least 1 hour before using. Refrigerate if not using that day.

Makes 1/2 cup dressing/marinade

Blueberries and Cream

When fresh blueberries are in season they are so luscious they need no other embellishment than a covering of fresh cream.

Lunch was so peaceful and inviting (page 42) there seemed no point in moving elsewhere for the evening meal.

Simple Sunday Supper

(page 42)

MENU
(for 6)

Chicken and Okra Gumbo

Pulled Bread with Sweet Butter

Arugula, Boston Lettuce, and
Julienne Red Pepper Salad

Pepocreme Cheese

Walnut Tart with Whipped Cream

Wine

Coffee

Chicken gumbo, rice, and chopped green onions.

Green salad with red pepper, and soft cheese.

A luscious walnut tart topped with whipped cream.

Simple Sunday Supper

This is one of the few menus that has a separate salad course. The soup doesn't seem quite enough alone. Dessert portions are very small.

Chicken and Okra Gumbo

There are dozens of recipes for gumbo using various methods. The one thing they all have in common is the roux, which gives the soup its distinctive flavor. The particular recipe here uses quite a large quantity of this robust element. The important thing to remember is to skim off the oil that rises to the top. The gumbo should be served over rice and can be garnished with chopped green onions if you like.

2	pounds chicken breasts, cut into 4 parts
2	pounds chicken thighs
	Salt, black pepper, and cayenne pepper to taste
	Oil for frying
1	cup chopped onion
1	cup chopped celery
4	cloves garlic, crushed
	Up to 1 cup oil
1	cup flour
2	quarts hot water
1	pound okra, tops and stems removed, cut into rings

Skin and season all the chicken pieces generously with salt and peppers. Brown them in about 1/2 inch of heated oil (vegetable or a combination of vegetable and bacon drippings). Remove to a large pot. Pour oil left after browning the chicken into a measuring cup. Add onion and celery to the pan and cook slowly until onion wilts. Add a little of the drained oil if necessary.

Scrape vegetables into pot with the chicken and add the garlic.

Add enough oil to that which was left over from cooking the chicken to measure 1 cup. Pour it, along with the flour, into a skillet to make the roux. Mix the flour together with the oil over medium heat. Use the reverse side of a flat-ended spatula to scrape the mixture from the bottom as it begins to brown. Keep it constantly moving. When it starts to brown it can go very quickly, so keep scraping it from the bottom and mixing. As the roux darkens you can lift the skillet from the heat and let it continue to cook from the retained heat. Remember that the browning process does not immediately stop when the skillet is removed from heat, so it is necessary to keep stirring. When the roux is about as dark as bread crust, it is almost ready. Darken it a bit more and immediately pour into the pot with the chicken and vegetables.

Pour 2 quarts hot water over all, and simmer slowly until the chicken is tender, over 1 hour. The soup should be rather thick, but thinner than pea soup. If it seems too thin, continue to simmer to reduce water content; if too thick, add a little more water and correct seasoning. During the cooking, oil will rise to the surface. Skim off as much of this as possible. When cooking is completed, allow soup to cool enough to remove the bones from the chicken. The soup can be made up to several days in advance and refrigerated. It is reheated to serve, with the okra being added during last 5 or 10 minutes. If it has been refrigerated, a bit more liquid may be needed.

To serve, put a scoop of rice into a bowl and pour the gumbo over it, making sure that everyone gets a few nice chunks of chicken and some okra.

Note: Peeled raw shrimp, oysters, or crabmeat may be added.

Serves 6

Pulled Bread

The name of this bread has nothing to do with its ingredients but rather with the way it is torn apart. Essentially, it is just shaggy pieces of bread that are toasted in the oven.

Use any large loaf of French or Italian bread. Pull it apart into tennis-ball-size pieces, cutting off all crust. Put on cookie sheet and toast in a 350-degree oven until brown. Serve with soft butter.

Arugula, Boston Lettuce, and Julienne Red Pepper Salad

Since arugula has a strong flavor, I like to combine it with a mild green like Boston lettuce. The strips of red pepper make it look appealing and add a bit of extra flavor. Serve with Pepocreme cheese, which has a mild Roquefort-like flavor and creamy texture.

- 1   bunch arugula
- 2   heads Boston lettuce
- 1   sweet red pepper, cut in julienne strips

Vinaigrette Dressing
- 2   tablespoons red wine vinegar
- 1   teaspoon salt, or to taste
- 1/4 teaspoon freshly ground black pepper
- 1   to 1 1/4 teaspoons dry mustard
- 3   tablespoons plus 1 teaspoon safflower oil
- 2   tablespoons mild olive oil

Wash and dry greens. Cut stems off arugula. Tear lettuce into bite-size pieces. Toss together with red pepper and keep covered in refrigerator until ready to serve.

To make dressing, whisk together vinegar, salt, pepper, and mustard. Then add oils and continue to whisk until smooth.

Makes 1/2 cup dressing

Walnut Tart with Whipped Cream

This tart can also be made in a regular 9-inch pie pan. If you make it in a rectangular 4 1/2 × 14 × 1-inch tart pan, as shown (which can be found in specialty food stores), put a sheet of lightly oiled foil between the outer tart frame and the bottom sheet to make it easier to remove it from the frame. During cooking time some of the liquid will also bubble out, but cooking it in a tart pan makes a very nice presentation.

Pie Crust
- 1 1/2 cups flour
-       Scant 1/4 teaspoon salt
- 6   tablespoons (3/4 stick) frozen unsalted butter, cut into 6 pieces
- 3   tablespoons frozen Crisco, cut into several pieces
- 4 1/2 to 5 tablespoons ice water

Filling
- 1 1/2 cups coarsely chopped walnuts
- 3   eggs
- 1   cup light corn syrup
- 1   tablespoon melted unsalted butter
- 1/2 teaspoon vanilla
- 1   tablespoon flour
- 1   cup sugar

Garnish
-       Walnut halves
- 1/2 pint whipping cream, flavored with 1 teaspoon vanilla

To make pastry, put flour and salt in a food processor. Add butter and Crisco. Process until the shortenings are the size of small peas. Add ice water and process until dough begins to cling together, not longer.

Gather dough into a ball and wrap in waxed paper. Refrigerate for 30 minutes. When ready to use, roll out and line the tart or pie pan. Trim the edges and return it to the refrigerator while preparing the filling.

Preheat oven to 375 degrees.

Put nuts in prepared pastry shell. Beat eggs and blend with the corn syrup, butter, and vanilla. Set aside. Combine flour and sugar and blend with the egg mixture. Pour mixture over nuts in pastry shell and let stand until nuts float to the top, so that they will glaze during baking. Trim with walnut halves if desired. Bake in the preheated oven 40 to 50 minutes, until filling is set and top browned. Serve with flavored whipped cream.

Serves 8

The bandannas in which this picnic lunch of bread, fruit, and cheese were tied do double duty as place mats at a roadside table. The parachute cloth canopy folds away to practically nothing and weighs very little.

MORE

LUNCHES

More Lunches

One of my favorite lunches, pictured on the previous page, is cheese, crusty bread, wine, and fruit. You could hardly ask for anything more satisfying and you will notice this combination at the center of many of my light noontime meals. The fact that such a little feast is so portable and transportable gives it an added plus. Try tying everything in bandannas or towels and take them along to be opened and enjoyed in any pleasant spot you come across—no mess and a minimum of spoilage.

Weekend guests love picnics, which is why three of the five lunches that follow are meals to be eaten away from the comforts of home. Since dining at the beach, especially, or on the water is no place like home, it is wise to keep this in mind when planning these outings. Make certain that your food-carrying containers have gaskets to make them leak-proof, or that the tops snap shut and stay firmly in place. If you enjoy this sort of dining, it's not a bad idea to make up a compact little kit of necessities such as salt, pepper, matches, corkscrew, aspirin, insect repellent, and the like, which you can just toss in with everything else. This is your permanent back-up kit and it should be left packed when you come home, ready for your next picnic. There is nothing worse than to need a safety pin or a bottle opener and have it be just out of reach. A word about flatware: If you are going to a location where there are no public disposal facilities—which means you will have to carry all your garbage home with you—I think you might just as well carry along something comfortable to eat with instead of disposable plastic utensils that break. Big plastic bags with twist ties are a good idea for empties or garbage and wet and/or sand-covered things. And incidentally, I'd rather have to deal with three or four medium-heavy totes than one or two heavy ones.

Remember that the food you prepare for an outing should be plentiful enough to take you through a whole day. Also remember that although beverages are rather heavy, people get dehydrated and are thirstier than they would be at home.

Vegetables are always an ingredient in my favorite home lunches, in almost any form—steamed, raw, hot, or cold (preferably just warm)—made into soup or fritters or a soufflé, dressed with vinaigrette, mayonnaise, an elegant herb concoction, or nothing at all. And, of course, vegetables combine beautifully with cheese and bread.

Whatever the food, in my view all lunches should be lazy affairs and be allowed to stretch on and on. That's why the menus to which I am most partial include extras for people to nibble at after the main part of the meal is finished. A relaxed lunch, with good conversation, can set the tone for the rest of the day.

Veal-stuffed red peppers with found objects.

Crackers and hard cheese for a snack later.

Crisp marinated vegetables.

54

Sour cream corn bread with a napkin collar to keep it in shape.

At the Beach

Suntan lotion is not enough for a day at the beach; a few creature comforts are a must.

At the Beach

MENU
(for 8)

Veal-Stuffed Red Sweet Peppers
Marinated Mixed Vegetables
Sour Cream Corn Bread
Fontina and Chaumes Cheese with Crackers
Assorted Plums
Walnut Cookies
Red Wine
Iced Tea

E ating at the beach can be comparable to finding yourself at a big buffet supper with a too-small plate overloaded with food in one hand and a napkin, knife and fork, and glass of wine in the other . . . and no place to sit. Only at the beach you have sand, too. Plan carefully and prepare simple, easy-to-eat foods that are neither too perishable nor too fragile. Also, because people are always hungry in sea air, the meal should be generous. Big napkins and premoistened towelettes are a great help. And make it red wine, which needn't be chilled.

This menu is based on the assumption that you have the marinated vegetables already prepared in your refrigerator. I usually do have a combination of some sort on hand for quick lunches and to eat with sandwiches. I would also plan to cook the peppers the day before, so that all I had to deal with on the day of the outing would be the corn bread, which takes only 45 minutes to cook. Although it keeps well for a day or so, it is best on the day it is cooked.

Veal-Stuffed Sweet Red Peppers

This recipe produces a rather dense stuffing. Any leftover cooked stuffing is good sliced thinly (this takes a very sharp knife) for open-face sandwiches. Use a thin, softish rye or whole-wheat bread spread with a bit of butter and mustard. Top with strips of the red pepper and sprinkle with capers.

8	medium sweet red peppers
2	pounds ground veal
3	teaspoons salt
1	teaspoon ground black pepper
2	tablespoons Worcestershire sauce
1½	cups finely chopped onion
2	cups cooked rice
4	tablespoons chopped parsley
1	egg

Freshly grated nutmeg (optional)

Preheat oven to 350 degrees.

Slice tops off stem end of peppers and clean out cavity. Even off bottoms so they will stand on end, being careful not to cut away so much that a hole is made. Add boiling water to just cover, parboil for 4 minutes, then hold in cold water.

Mix all the remaining ingredients except egg and nutmeg. This is best done with the hands. Beat egg lightly and incorporate.

Drain peppers and put a kettle of water on to boil. Dry interiors of the peppers and pack with stuffing, finishing off with a mounded top. Put them in a greased ovenproof dish into which they fit snugly. Sprinkle tops of each generously with salt and pepper (and a touch of nutmeg if you like). Pour boiling water into pan to come halfway up the sides of the peppers. Cover loosely with foil and bake for approximately 45 minutes. Remove foil to finish. Total cooking time is from 1 to 1¼ hours. Remove from pan to a rack to cool. Do not refrigerate.

Serves 8

Marinated Mixed Vegetables

This combination of vegetables is one I like personally, but any hard vegetable can be used. You can even add button mushrooms.

1	very small head cauliflower, in florets
1	large package frozen lima beans, cooked 4 minutes
3	carrots, cut into rings
1	large green pepper, cut into strips
1/2	pound green beans, ends snapped off and cut into pieces
1	large zucchini, cut into strips

Marinade

3	cloves garlic, crushed
1	cup safflower oil
1 3/4	cups wine vinegar
1/3	cup sugar
2	teaspoons salt, or to taste
2	teaspoons dry mustard
	Freshly ground black pepper to taste

Put vegetables into a refrigerator container with a cover. Mix all ingredients of the marinade and pour into the container with the vegetables. This will probably not cover all the vegetables but don't worry, they will settle. Marinate for at least 48 hours. Stir once or twice.

Serves 8

Sour Cream Corn Bread

This corn bread is very tender right after it is first baked, so it should be allowed to cool 10 minutes before cutting. It is good at room temperature, as it remains quite moist. Do not refrigerate leftovers.

2/3	cup safflower oil
2	eggs, lightly beaten
1	8-ounce container sour cream
1	16-ounce can creamed corn
1	medium onion, grated
1 1/2	cups yellow cornmeal
2	teaspoons baking powder
1	teaspoon salt
1	cup grated sharp Cheddar cheese

Preheat oven to 350 degrees. Oil a 9-inch round iron skillet or heavy pan.

Mix safflower oil, eggs, sour cream, and creamed corn. Mix in the grated onion.

Mix the dry ingredients and pour the liquid ingredients in. Mix quickly; the batter should be a bit lumpy. Pour half the batter into the prepared pan. Sprinkle it with 3/4 cup cheese. Carefully pour remaining batter over the cheese layer. Top with the remaining 1/4 cup cheese. Bake for 45 minutes. Cut in wedges to serve.

Serves 8

Walnut Cookies

This is a wafer cookie. As with most thin cookies, the important thing here is the consistency of the dough. It should not fall from the spoon but should be thick enough so that you must force it out with another spoon. If too thin, add another tablespoon or more of flour.

1 1/2	cups brown sugar, firmly packed
1/2	teaspoon vanilla
1/2	cup (1 stick) unsalted butter
1	cup flour, unsifted
1	cup finely chopped walnuts

Preheat oven to 350 degrees.

Put 1/2 cup sugar and 1/2 cup water in a pan and boil for 3 minutes. Remove from heat and add the vanilla and butter. Let stand until the butter melts. Add the remaining sugar, flour, and nuts, mixing well after each addition.

Drop by tablespoons on a well-buttered cookie sheet, leaving 2 inches in between. Bake for 8 to 9 minutes. Allow to cool a few minutes before removing with a spatula.

Makes 2 dozen cookies

Right: *Use a large low basket for "tailgate" picnics—it doesn't have to be unpacked and then repacked later. Leave this traveling buffet out for whenever people get hungry.*

MENU
(for 6)

Chicken, Leek, and Carrot Loaf
Fried French Bread Slices
Refrigerator-Pickled Broccoli
Baked Green Rice
Cherry Tomatoes, Black Olives,
and Green Onions
Vermont White Cheddar Cheese
Jam and Berry Tarts
Wine
Iced Tea

Little tarts—perfect for eating with the hands.

For an Outdoor Event

For an Outdoor Event

The most important thing about such a lunch is the ease with which it can be transported and eaten. None of these dishes includes mayonnaise or any other ingredient that will spoil too readily, and all can stand a little mistreatment on the way. By putting slices of chicken loaf on pieces of fried French bread, they can be eaten without a plate and with a minimum of mess. Big napkins are a must. I use dish towels for picnic napkins.

Chicken, Leek, and Carrot Loaf

The combination of vegetables and herbs used with this chicken dish is rather classic, and for that reason it will have a familiar flavor. After you have tried it this way, why not use a less traditional combination? For instance, beets, red onions, and fresh sage might be interesting with chicken instead of the leeks, carrots, and tarragon.

- 1½ pounds boned chicken breast
- 1   or more tablespoons safflower oil
- ½   cup carrots, cut into rings
- 1   cup leeks, cut into ½-inch rings
- 1   teaspoon salt
- ¼   teaspoon black pepper
- ¼   teaspoon savory
- 2   tablespoons minced fresh parsley
- 1   tablespoon minced fresh tarragon or 1 teaspoon dried
- 1   egg

Preheat the oven to 375 degrees. Put a kettle of water on to boil.

Grind the chicken lightly, or chop in a food processor. Do not overgrind, as the meat is very tender. Set aside.

In 1 tablespoon safflower oil sauté carrots for several minutes; add leeks, and continue to cook slowly until leeks are wilted. More oil may be added if necessary. Set aside.

Put chicken in a large bowl and add the cooked vegetables. Mix well. Add all other ingredients except egg and mix well again. Beat egg lightly and mix with other ingredients.

Pour into a 4 × 5-inch ceramic pâté loaf pan, then put it in a slightly larger baking dish. Pour in enough boiling water to come about ½ inch up the sides of the loaf pan. Bake for 1¼ hours. Take out of oven and allow to cool in pan for 30 minutes. Run a knife around edge and invert on platter to cool further. Be careful when pan is inverted, as there will be liquid in it.

Serves 6

Fried French Bread Slices

Bread done this way stays crisp. It also makes a firm base on which to build an open sandwich to be eaten with your hands if you like.

- ½   cup (1 stick) unsalted butter, melted and clarified
- 4   tablespoons olive oil
- 1   large loaf French or Italian bread, cut into ½-inch slices

Mix the clarified butter and oil. Carefully and generously paint one side of the bread slices with the mixture. Put them, painted side down, into a cold skillet. Turn to medium heat. (They will not all fit at one time, so let the skillet cool a minute before starting the second batch.) While slices are browning on the underside, paint their top sides with the butter and oil. Turn and brown. Repeat until all the bread is browned on both sides. Use more butter if necessary. Do not refrigerate.

Serves 6

Refrigerator-Pickled Broccoli

These pickles are simple to make and will keep for weeks in a covered container in the refrigerator.

- ⅔   cup cider vinegar
- ⅓   cup olive oil
- ¼   cup Pommery mustard
- 2   tablespoons honey

½ teaspoon curry powder
Salt to taste
4 cups broccoli florets
½ medium green pepper, cut into ¼-inch strips 1 inch long

Whisk together vinegar, oil, mustard, honey, and curry. Add salt and set aside.

Blanch broccoli in boiling water for 2 to 3 minutes. Drain and transfer to a glass container. Pour in marinade and lay green pepper strips on top. Cover container and allow to cool. Refrigerate for 48 hours before using.

Serves 6

Baked Green Rice

This loaf will be easy to slice when it really cools down and the cheese has had a chance to set. Bake it in a loaf pan so that the slices will be regular and will pack neatly.

2 cups cooked rice (approximately 1¼ cups uncooked)
1 4-ounce can chopped green chili peppers (not hot)
1 small onion, chopped fine
2 cups grated Cheddar cheese
1 cup finely chopped parsley
1 cup melted unsalted butter
2 eggs
1 cup milk

Preheat oven to 350 degrees. Grease a 4 × 5-inch ceramic pâté loaf pan lightly and line the bottom with waxed paper, then grease paper lightly.

Combine the rice, chili peppers, onion, cheese, and parsley. Mix well. Add melted butter and mix. Beat eggs lightly and add the milk. Stir and add to the other ingredients. Mix thoroughly.

Pour into the pan and bake for 40 to 45 minutes. Allow to cool completely, loosen sides, and turn out. Remove waxed paper. Use a very sharp knife and cut into slices.

Serves 6

Jam and Berry Tarts

These tarts are best eaten with your hands, so take along a few paper towels to wrap them in. It is also a good idea to add buttered soft bread crumbs to the filling mixture so that it won't be runny when you bite into it. Almost any kind of jam can be combined with berries and/or grated lemon rind. Fig Conserve (page 41) and fresh raspberries would be a luscious combination.

1½ cups flour
1 tablespoon sugar
6 tablespoons (¾ stick) frozen butter
4 tablespoons frozen Crisco
5 to 6 tablespoons ice water
1 cup tangerine marmalade
½ cup soft bread crumbs, mixed with melted butter
12 strawberries, sliced if large

Preheat oven to 350 degrees. Lightly grease a cookie sheet.

Combine flour, sugar, and a pinch of salt in a food processor fitted with a metal blade. Turn off and on a few times. Add the frozen butter and Crisco. Process until the shortening is the size of small peas. Add 5 tablespoons ice water. Process until dough begins to form a ball; remove before it does. (More water might be added if necessary.) Gather into a ball, dust with flour, and refrigerate in plastic wrap for 30 minutes.

When ready to use, roll out half the dough into a thin sheet. Have ready the marmalade mixed with the soft buttered bread crumbs. If you have a tart maker, heap a tablespoon of the jam-crumb mixture onto the center of a 5-inch square of rolled-out dough. Top with a berry or two. Place another square of pastry on top of this. Cut and seal with the tart maker. Remove to the cookie sheet and sprinkle the top generously with granulated sugar. When the first sheet of dough is used, repeat with the second.

If you don't have a tart maker, use the same square, but put the filling in one side and fold the dough over on itself. Seal the three open sides by pressing them together with the tines of a fork. You will then have a tart shaped vaguely like a hotdog bun. Bake until golden, about 20 to 25 minutes. Remove to a rack to cool.

Makes 8 tarts

Marinated shrimp with fresh corn.

Steamed okra ready to be dressed with a tomato vinaigrette.

In the Meadow

If you hit one of those cloudy, warm days, take advantage of it by moving everything outdoors and enjoying the beautiful vistas. The soft light makes everything, including you and your guests, look great—this should be enough to soothe anyone who might tend to hold you responsible for the weather.

Plump green figs.

Everything set out on a table with a seersucker cover.

In the Meadow

> ## MENU
> *(for 6)*
>
> *Marinated Shrimp and Fresh Corn*
> *Steamed Okra with Tomato Vinaigrette*
> *Boiled New Potatoes*
> *Green Olives*
> *Thin-Sliced Dark Bread and Sweet Butter*
> *Layered Mascarpone and Gorgonzola Cheese*
> *Fresh Figs*
> *Wine*
> *Iced tea*

When preparing this lunch, fix the shrimp first because it must marinate. You can even make it a day in advance if you have the time. The vegetables can be cooked when you are in the mood. If you like, you can substitute other vegetables for the ones I have suggested to accompany the shrimp and corn dish. Whatever you use, make sure to give the cooked vegetables time to cool down and the cheese time to warm up to room temperature before serving.

If your table is a good distance from the house, you might make transporting the food simpler by combining the vegetables into one dish—for instance, a rice salad with tomatoes and olives and green peas in place of separate dishes of okra and potatoes. I don't ordinarily like two mixed salads of equal importance (the shrimp is really a salad) served together—I would rather have one hearty salad served with a few individual steamed vegetables—but sometimes convenience wins out.

Marinated Shrimp and Fresh Corn

There are simple devices that you can buy at most fish stores to devein and shuck shrimp. They save a lot of time, so are worth the money.

36	medium to large shrimp
	Shrimp and crab boil (prepacked, mixed seasoning)
1½	cups (or more) fresh corn kernels

Marinade

1	large egg yolk
¾	cup olive oil
¾	cup peanut oil
¾	cup red wine vinegar
3	tablespoons Dijon mustard
3	tablespoons chopped chives
3	tablespoons chopped parsley
1	tablespoon chopped shallots

Devein and peel shrimp. Cover with water in a saucepan and put in several tablespoons of shrimp and crab boil. Bring to a boil. They will turn pink in just a few minutes. Turn off and allow to cool in the water.

Steam the corn kernels for 2 minutes. Set aside.

Whisk together the egg yolk, oils, vinegar, and mustard. Add chives, parsley, and shallots.

Drain the shrimp and put in a serving bowl. Pour the marinade over it. Refrigerate for at least 2 hours, turning several times. Refrigerate the corn separately and add to the mixture when you are ready to serve.

Serves 6

Steamed Okra with Tomato Vinaigrette

The truth is you don't really need this dish as a part of this menu. It is just a nice extra if you have the time. The wonderful warm vinaigrette is good on any steamed vegetable.

1   pound okra, tops and tips trimmed

Tomato Vinaigrette

- 4   tablespoons olive oil
- 4   tablespoons shallots, finely chopped
- 1   cup tomatoes, peeled, seeded, and chopped
- 4   tablespoons red wine vinegar
- 1   clove garlic, finely chopped
- 2/3   cup dry white wine
- 1/4   teaspoon salt
-     Freshly ground pepper to taste
- 2   tablespoons chopped gherkins
- 3   tablespoons small capers (or large, chopped), drained

Steam okra for 5 minutes, or until just fork tender. Allow to cool. Do not refrigerate.

Heat the oil and add the shallots; cook until wilted. Add tomatoes and simmer for approximately 5 minutes. Add vinegar, garlic, wine, salt, and pepper. Simmer for 15 to 20 minutes, or until reduced to a thick sauce. Correct seasoning. Add gherkins and capers and serve warm over the okra.

Serves 6

Boiled New Potatoes

Try to get very small, red, new potatoes if they are available. They should be no larger than small to medium.

Scrub 2 pounds potatoes, put in a saucepan, and cover with water. Add a teaspoon of salt. Simmer until fork tender. Depending on their size, cooking time will be 15 minutes or longer.

Layered Mascarpone and Gorgonzola Cheese

This cheese is sometimes referred to as a "Mascarpone Tart." It is also available with basil, but I like it better plain.

Mascarpone cheese has only recently become generally available in this country. By itself it has a very mild flavor and a wonderfully smooth texture. I once had it in Italy as a filling in a dessert crepe. It is also sold layered with chopped dried figs and pine nuts, which makes a lovely dessert when served with thin, lightly sweetened crackers and wine.

If you can't find the "tart" in your area, ask for a soft, mild blue cheese. Pepocreme, which is mentioned elsewhere in this book, is one such. Or try Bleu de Bresse.

Fresh Figs

Allow 2 or 3 figs per person if they are large, more if they are small and you have fig fanciers visiting.

If you like figs but live in an area where they don't grow outdoors, you might want to plant one or two of the miniature varieties in tubs that can be wheeled into a sunny room for the winter. They grow nicely under these conditions and make a very pretty plant.

Actually I have several plants that I grow outside in the ground (on Long Island). They are espaliered against the house, and after the leaves have fallen off I surround their roots with salt-hay and tack old strips of burlap across the plants. I then stuff more hay around the upper part of the plants inside the burlap. This might seem like a chore, but it doesn't really take too much effort, and when you consider the cost of a few figs, it is worth the time.

On the Water

As you can see, for this picnic we tied up everything that wouldn't fit into the ice chest—several varieties of plums, dried apricots, a loaf of sliced and buttered bread, and raspberry jam cake—in large dish towels. This considerably simplified the unloading and protected the food from sand and pebbles, too. After the meal, we just tied up the leftovers the same way. The sesame chicken breasts with lemon had their own little carrying box.

On the Water

I would put this whole picnic together right after breakfast to give everything time to get to the right temperature. The chicken needs to marinate a bit, but the cooking time is very brief. Vegetables can be covered with ice water to crisp at some point along the way. The cake would be made in advance. As a matter of fact, the white beans could be cooked the day before (and refrigerated), to be dressed the next morning.

Sesame Chicken Breasts

I am very fond of the flavor of sesame oil, but it has to be used sparingly because it is so potent. This recipe was devised by our photographer, Joshua Greene.

6 tablespoons soy sauce
1/4 cup water
2 tablespoons sesame oil
 Juice and scrapings from grating of 3-inch piece of ginger root, unpeeled (use the fine grating side)
 Juice of 2 1/2 lemons
3 large chicken breasts, skinned, boned, and cut in two
 Toasted sesame seeds (enough to make single layer on cookie sheet)

 Lemon slices

Mix the soy sauce, water, sesame oil, ginger juice and scrapings, and lemon juice in a glass bowl large enough to hold the chicken breasts comfortably. You should have 6 ounces or more of marinade. If not, add enough water to make up the difference. Put the chicken into the mixture, cover with plastic wrap, and refrigerate for at least 1 hour. Turn a few times if the marinade doesn't quite cover the breasts.

When ready, broil the breasts in a preheated broiler for approximately 8 to 10 minutes per side. This will vary with the thickness of the meat. Baste with the marinade a few times during the cooking. Test for doneness by cutting into one of the pieces. Remove to a platter.

Spread a layer of toasted sesame seeds on a sheet of waxed paper and roll the cooked breasts in them, carefully coating both sides. Serve at room temperature, garnished with lemon slices. Do not refrigerate.

Serves 6

Whole-Grain Bread and Sweet Butter

Buy a loaf of unsliced whole-grain bread and cut it into thick slices. Butter very generously with soft sweet butter and reassemble the loaf. Tie together with a large cloth napkin or dish towel.

White Beans Vinaigrette

You could add any number of crunchy or aromatic vegetables to white beans and dress them simply with olive oil and wine vinegar, but my favorite combination is this one of beans, chopped, roasted red sweet peppers, and parsley with a simple vinaigrette. You may also add green onions, green pepper, and peeled and seeded cucumber.

1 package dried navy beans
1 medium onion, peeled and stuck with 4 cloves
1 bay leaf
1 1-inch piece salt pork
  Salt and pepper to taste
1 roasted red pepper, chopped
3 or 4 sprigs parsley, finely chopped

Vinaigrette Dressing

1 teaspoon salt, or to taste
1 generous teaspoon Dijon mustard
  Scant 1/4 teaspoon black pepper
2 tablespoons red wine vinegar
3 tablespoons safflower oil
2 tablespoons mild olive oil

Wash beans in cold water and pick over to remove any stems or odd pieces. Put in a pot on the stove, cover with boiling water, and bring back to a boil. Simmer for 1 minute. Turn the heat off and allow them to sit for one hour. Drain.

Cover beans with fresh water and add the onion, bay leaf, salt pork, salt and pepper. Simmer uncovered until done, approximately 1 1/2 hours. Drain, discarding everything but the beans. Allow to cool.

Whisk together all ingredients for vinaigrette except the oils. Add them and continue to whisk until smooth. Combine the red pepper and parsley with the beans and toss with dressing. Serve at room temperature. Store in refrigerator if not using immediately.

Serves 6

Raw Vegetables on Ice

Cut celery, carrots, and green peppers into strips of even length. Cut the root and top off green onions, leaving a little of the green. Wash and cut into even lengths. Wash radishes, and cut top and root off. Remove stems from pear tomatoes and wash.

Serve all vegetables on a bed of crushed ice.

Black Raspberry Cake

This cake is dense and the perfect kind to take on an outing where it might get a bit of rough handling. The recipe for it was given to me by a friend, Jean Thackery, who says it was one of her family favorites. Now it is one of my favorites. Here, it should simply be washed down with iced tea. For at-home occasions it is good with whipped cream or ice cream and afternoon tea.

1/2 cup (1 stick) unsalted butter
1 cup light brown sugar, tightly packed
3 eggs
2 cups sifted cake flour
1/2 teaspoon baking soda
2 teaspoons baking powder
1 teaspoon nutmeg
1/4 teaspoon ground cloves
1/2 teaspoon cinnamon
1 cup pure seedless black raspberry jam
1/3 cup sour cream

Preheat oven to 375 degrees.

Butter a piece of waxed paper to fit into the bottom of a lightly greased 9-inch tube pan. Grease the paper slightly.

Cream butter and add the sugar gradually. Beat until light and fluffy. Separate the eggs. Set the whites aside and add the yolks to the butter-sugar mixture. Mix well.

Sift together the dry ingredients and add to butter-sugar mixture alternately with the combined jam and sour cream. Beat the egg whites until stiff and fold in with an over-and-under motion. Pour into the pan and bake for 45 to 50 minutes. Allow to cool slightly, then run a knife around the edge of the pan and turn out. Remove the waxed paper.

Makes one 9-inch tube cake

Black Forest ham and tomatoes.

Rice with eggs and vegetables and grated Parmesan.

By the Pool

The shady end of this beautiful black pool is a perfect spot for a lazy Sunday lunch. The menu couldn't be simpler or easier: thin slices of Black Forest ham, rolled to be eaten with the fingers; red ripe tomatoes with homemade mayonnaise; a chunky eggplant and red pepper condiment; French bread and sweet butter; a kind of simple fried rice dish topped with Parmesan cheese; and, for dessert, two kinds of watermelon.

Sweet red pepper and eggplant condiment.

Yellow and red watermelon.

By the Pool

The wonderful Sweet Red Pepper and Eggplant Condiment in this menu lasts for several weeks in the refrigerator, so it would be on hand. The ham can be store bought and is delicious. You only have to roll each of the thin slices so that they will be easier to serve and eat. Mayonnaise is a staple (see recipe page 153). Melon balls are simple to make but could just be chunks instead of balls. This leaves only the egg dish, which can be made in 10 or 15 minutes.

MENU
(for 6)

Thinly Sliced Black Forest Ham
Rice with Eggs and Vegetables
Sweet Red Pepper and Eggplant Condiment
Sliced Tomatoes with Mayonnaise
French Bread and Butter
Watermelon Balls
Iced Tea
Wine

This is a good lunch to prepare when you have had just about enough cooking for one weekend. It is not a bad idea to have several easy-to-do menus in the back of your head for just such times. If you are not in the mood for cooking, there is nothing worse than having to do a meal from scratch, especially when you would rather be relaxing by the pool or at the beach.

If you happen to have guests who like to cook, don't be shy about asking one of them to make a lunch for the group. If you do, it is wise (at the same time) to get someone to say they will clean up afterward. People tend to be awfully messy in someone else's kitchen. This must have something to do with their being in unfamiliar territory. The second worst thing to have to do when you would rather be elsewhere is to clean up after a meal you didn't cook.

Rice with Eggs and Vegetables

This rice concoction resembles Chinese fried rice and can be cooked to any degree of doneness if the vegetables have been slightly wilted first.

2	tablespoons safflower oil
3/4	cup finely chopped sweet red pepper
3/4	cup finely chopped green onions, including some top
4	cups cooked rice (cooked in chicken stock)
3	large eggs
1/2	teaspoon salt
	Freshly ground black pepper to taste
2	tablespoons clarified unsalted butter
1/4	pound Parmesan cheese, grated

Heat 1 tablespoon of safflower oil in a large skillet and add the pepper and the onions. Sauté slowly until just wilted. Add the rice and mix.

In a large bowl, beat the eggs and add the salt and pepper. Add the rice-vegetable mixture in and mix well.

Wipe out the skillet and add the remaining oil and the butter. When foamy, add the egg-rice and cook, turning until the eggs are set. Make sure it is turned and separated so that all the egg has a chance to cook. Heap onto a serving plate and serve with grated Parmesan cheese on the side.

Serves 6

Sweet Red Pepper and Eggplant Condiment

When red peppers are plentiful I always keep a supply of this delicious condiment on hand to serve with eggs and to pep up lunches of leftovers. It is delicious with goat cheese, crusty bread, and a tomato or two. This keeps several weeks, tightly covered, in the refrigerator.

1	cup chicken stock
1	pound small eggplants
4	large red peppers
3	tablespoons safflower oil
1	tablespoon sesame oil
2	tablespoons dark soy sauce
½	a small dried Chinese red pepper, finely chopped
2	tablespoons pale dry sherry
1½	teaspoons sugar

Put the chicken stock on to warm.

Trim the ends of the eggplant and cut each into thin strips, about ½ inch wide. Core the red pepper and cut into strips the same size as the eggplant.

Heat the oils in a large skillet and sauté eggplant and peppers over medium-high heat, stirring lightly all the while. Continue for about 5 minutes. Add heated stock and all the other ingredients, mix, and simmer for 8 to 10 minutes. Allow to cool and refrigerate. This is better if it has a day to marinate.

Makes approximately 1 pint

Watermelon Balls

For me, as well as for most people, watermelon is practically synonymous with summer. Luckily, small varieties that take up much less space in crowded refrigerators are now widely available. There are also varieties that are a beautiful shade of yellow on the inside. The contrasting colors and textures of red and yellow watermelon balls are a treat for the taste buds as well as the eyes—and they make a spectacular presentation for company.

74

"No-Work" Lunches

"No-Work" Lunches

These lunches, and the fruit desserts that follow, have a very strong element in common—the way they look. The light in the open shaded area where I usually dine at noon seems to intensify the color of everything, and I am constantly struck by how beautiful it all looks on the plate. I am so partial to fresh and mostly uncooked produce that several bright, clear colors are always there—transparent thin-sliced red onion, green asparagus, leeks turned saffron-colored by chicken stock—all accompanied by shiny olives, creamy cheese, and rich-textured bread. The tempting beauty of all these things is enough to convert even a confirmed meat-and-potatoes person. The same is true of the fruit in the fruit desserts. In its natural state fruit can be as breathtaking a visual treat as any food you might choose to prepare.

I'm not going to spell out exactly how to make these speedy little lunches, because the point is to use whatever is on hand. The great thing they all have in common is that they don't (and shouldn't) take more than 15 or 20 minutes to prepare.

Always keep a supply of breads (they freeze well) and cheese, olives, pickles, and assorted condiments, both ones bought and those prepared by you. Things like wilted onions, pickled beets, roasted sweet red peppers in olive oil, good mustards, vinaigrette, and homemade mayonnaise do wonders for a thrown-together meal. So do fresh green onions, buttered radishes, and strips of bell pepper. You just must decide early enough what you are going to use so that everything that should be, can come to room temperature.

It gets down to simply using what is there and not doing anything special. For instance, chicken breasts and leeks could easily be simmered together in just 15 minutes (not counting the cooling time) and could even be done along with those cooked for another meal. Just remember to do it at the time. Or suppose you have some cold baked macaroni and cheese. Slice and let it warm up. Set it on a bed of chopped lettuce and watercress (plus any other salad green you might have around), which you have dressed ever so lightly with a vinaigrette. Should you find yourself with a small quantity of ham or a few pieces of bacon, chop it and sprinkle it over the pasta and snip a few chives over that, or some parsley if you have it. Make a sauce of mayonnaise, mustard, caper, pickles, and dill to serve on the side. Add a few ubiquitous tomatoes, some black olives, and toasted crackers. You could keep going . . . hard-boil a couple of eggs and put an anchovy fillet on top of each slice. Do you have roasted peppers? Why not add them, too. Make do! Look in the refrigerator and cabinets. Use your imagination. Don't let anything escape.

· 1 ·

Vegetable fritters with chutney
Sour pickles   Mustard
Green onions   Cherry tomatoes

You may use any leftover vegetables to make these fritters. I like to combine several of them. Just chop all the vegetables coarsely and add to a simple fritter batter recipe found in any basic cookbook. Serve with chutney, mustard, and pickles, garnished with cherry tomatoes and green onions.

· 2 ·

Asparagus with butter
Hard-boiled eggs with chives
Soft cheese   French bread

When fresh asparagus first becomes available in the spring, I like to have a lunch of nothing else but. Here I have added a hard-boiled egg topped with fresh chives and some cheese.

· 3 ·

Poached chicken breasts   Leeks
Tomato slices   Black olives   French bread

Bone and skin small chicken breasts. Wash several small leeks carefully, as on page 116. Put the chicken breasts, which have been cut in two, and the leeks into a pot. Cover with chicken stock and simmer until tender. Allow to cool in the stock. (Reserve the stock for making soup.)

Serve the breasts with fresh mayonnaise, peeled and sliced tomatoes, French bread, and black olives dressed with olive oil and herbs (see page 33).

• 4 •

Pancetta bacon
Roasted red pepper
New potatoes and red onion rings
Pear tomatoes
Country white bread   Firm cheese

Pancetta is an uncured Italian bacon. Have it sliced thick and fry it like regular bacon. Boil the new potatoes in their skins and serve with Strong Vinaigrette (see recipe page 153), bread, cheese, onion rings, and tomatoes.

• 5 •

Escarole soup with
grated Parmesan cheese
Dark bread with sweet butter

To make this soup, use a strong chicken stock or the stock in which you have poached leeks (see page 161) and add escarole torn into small pieces. Simmer for 15 to 20 minutes.

• 6 •

Open-face egg salad sandwiches with chives
Green olives   Sliced tomatoes
Goat cheese with black pepper

The secret to good egg salad is the texture of the chopped egg. Some people are very careless about this. The egg must either be chopped *very*, very fine or put through a hand ricer, which is what I use. If you don't do this, when you add the mayonnaise—which should always be homemade—the yolks dissolve, leaving big chunks of white. Add a snip of fresh chives and salt and pepper to taste. Be cautious when adding the salt; it is easy to overdo.

I like egg salad on heavy-texture dark bread, either toasted or plain. Toasted, the sandwiches are easier to eat open-face. Serve with peeled and sliced tomatoes; plain green unpitted olives; and mild goat (Chevre) cheese, cut in rings and topped with a generous grind of fresh pepper.

• 7 •

Vegetable soup   Black bread
Firm cheese   Red onion rings

Make this vegetable soup by first browning chopped onion, celery, and carrots in a little safflower oil. Add boiling water and any combination of fresh vegetables you like, making sure that one of them is a starch, like potatoes or navy beans (or rice or small pasta), and another is tomatoes. It is preferable to use fresh tomatoes, but crushed canned ones will do. Simmer for 30 minutes or so, skimming occasionally. Add salt and pepper midway through the cooking time.

Serve with cheese—good white Vermont Cheddar is nice with the soup—black bread, and red onion rings.

• 8 •

Open-face bacon, lettuce,
and tomato sandwiches
Black olives   Green onions   Corn salad

Make sure the toast is well-browned, the tomatoes are the freshest, the lettuce is crisp, and the mayonnaise is homemade. For the salad, cut kernels off any leftover ears of steamed corn and dress with a light Vinaigrette (see recipe page 49). You may also add snipped chives or chopped green peppers and pimento if that appeals to you.

• 9 •

Sliced tomatoes with wilted red onions
Black olives   Soft cheese   Whole-grain bread

Plunge medium-size tomatoes into hot water for 8 to 10 seconds to make them easier to peel. Cut into slices and top with Wilted Red Onions (see recipe page 100). The black olives are dressed with olive oil and herbs, as on page 33. The cheese should be one of the soft blues.

Natural
Fruit
Desserts

Natural Fruit Desserts

Aside from their visual impact, these desserts are vastly appealing because they need no refined sugar. Of course, you could add a small quantity of some artificial sweetener or tart them up with a bit of something like Grand Marnier, but they really can stand on their own. They should, of course, be made when fruit is at the height of its season and therefore filled with natural sugar, and always be topped with a purée and some sort of citrus grating or zest. It is surprising how much these two elements add to the overall taste of the finished dessert, especially the small bits of sharp citrus.

When making a purée, I usually use two kinds of fruit mixed. One can be dried if you like. Also important is lemon, lime, or orange juice—freshly squeezed only. I don't use grated lime skin often because it can be bitter instead of zesty. Some fruits such as peaches or pears should be rubbed with lemon juice as soon as they are peeled (or skinned) to keep them from turning dark. A delicious purée can be made from ripe pears and dried apricots, with lemon juice. Another beautiful and delectable one is made from strawberries and blueberries with lemon juice.

Composing these desserts is like composing a picture. Have all the elements handy and get to work, tasting as you go. Make notes on combinations you like. It is easy to forget a key ingredient, and for these to be right, every element is important.

• 1 •

Bananas and raspberries
Purée of dried pineapple, raspberries, and orange juice
Thin orange-rind strips, grated lemon rind, and tiny slices of dried pineapple

Select a small- to medium-size firm banana with a bright yellow unblemished skin. Cut off its two ends neatly and peel. Cut in two, lengthwise, and cut each of these portions in two. Use the largest red raspberries you can find. Save any misshapen or slightly crushed berries to use in the purée.

• 2 •

Pineapple and champagne grapes
Purée of strawberries and lemon juice
Grated lemon rind and freshly grated nutmeg

Buy a small, very ripe pineapple without any soft spots and cut off the top and bottom. Peel off the brown skin, cutting fairly deep. Remove any brown "eyes" that may remain. Cut into rings.

Use champagne grapes, a small seedless variety that often appears in the summer and is translucently brownish red in color with a wonderfully sweet flavor. These grapes are often expensive, but you won't need many. Sort out any bruised ones and use them later in a compote with bananas.

• 3 •

Peach, blueberries, and dried figs
Purée of blueberries, dried figs, and lemon juice
Grated lemon rind

Use a perfect peach of good size. Make sure there are no soft spots in it as these are often brown under the skin. Dip the peach in boiling water for 30 seconds. The skin will slip right off. Cut into two halves and carefully loosen the pit and remove. Bathe the halves in lemon juice as soon as they are peeled and pitted to keep them from turning brown. Use large perfect blueberries; damaged ones can be used in the purée.

• 4 •

Grapefruit
Purée of blueberries, dried pear,
and lemon juice
Small cubes of dried pear, lemon strips,
and chopped walnuts

Peel a medium-size grapefruit and plunge into
boiling water for 15 seconds to make it easier to
peel off the thick white layer underneath the outer
skin. Divide into sections, and using a sharp knife
(which will be made dull by the citrus juice) peel
the membrane from each section. If one or two of
these sections should break in two, they can be put
back together on the plate.

• 5 •

Fresh figs
Purée of dried apples, dried dates,
orange, and lemon juice
Small strips of orange rind, grated
lemon rind, and slivers of date

If you are using the small brown variety of fig
shown in the photograph, wash and dry them
thoroughly and cut off the stems. Cut each in half.
If you are using the larger green variety, be more
careful in selecting them as they tend to damage
more easily; they should be peeled and cut into
four parts.

The purée is very heavy, so it should be used
sparingly.

• 6 •

Yellow watermelon and blackberries
Purée of peaches and lemon juice
Strips of lemon rind and
slivers of fresh mint

Select a small yellow pulped watermelon and cut
it through the middle so that you can make rounds
½ inch thick. Carefully cut away the outer skin
and the sour white portion under the skin,
preserving the circular shape. Cut the circle into
wedge shapes and remove the black seeds. Rinse
and dry large blueberries, using only the perfect
ones. Set aside any damaged or bruised berries to
be used in another purée.

• 7 •

Honeydew or other green melon
Purée of fresh pear, dried apricots,
and lemon juice
Tiny slivers of dried apricot
and grated lemon rind

Select a small ripe melon with no soft
indentations. Cut it in two and remove the seeds
and any loose or stringy pulp. Cut into 8 to 10
slices (depending on the size), and peel the rind off
along with about a quarter inch of the pulp to get
rid of any residue of the bitter rind.

• 8 •

Red plum, orange, and blueberries
Purée of red raspberries, blueberries,
plum pulp, and orange juice
Grated lemon rind and nutmeg

Peel a good-size red plum and slice it on both sides
until you come to the pit. Cut off any pulp that is
still clinging to the pit to use in the purée. Peel a
medium-size naval orange and plunge into boiling
water for about 15 seconds. This will make it
easier to remove the thick white portion of skin
still clinging to the fruit.

Spice applesauce cake.

Lord Baltimore cake.

Meringue nut cookies.

Treats and Surprises

I have a childhood memory of certain Sunday suppers being made up solely of a thrilling treat—great quantities of hand-turned ice cream full of fresh strawberries or peaches, accompanied by a spectacular white layer cake piled with boiled icing. Such splendid excess would have been too much after our traditional big Sunday midday meal, so it became a meal in itself in the evening. I don't think I ever got through these times without getting dessert all over my face. Oh happy memory! Probably it is this very memory that accounts for my fondness for desserts served at odd times as "treats," instead of following a meal. I especially like to serve these on afternoons when it rains unexpectedly or on a day that suddenly turns cold.

I am partial to tea in the afternoon; I find it both a relaxant and a restorative. Most guests seem to agree. Served alone it is refreshing, but who would want to refuse a sliver (or two) of dark and moist applesauce cake if it just happens to be there? Or what about a slice of old-fashioned Lord Baltimore cake with its ridiculously wonderful icing?

The recipes that follow have nothing in particular in common beyond the fact that they are favorites of mine (and my guests). They are also a good way to make use of those leftover egg whites and yolks that you can't seem to bring yourself to throw away.

Strawberry shortcake.

Treats and Surprises

Spice Applesauce Cake

This recipe came to me via a friend who saw it in a newspaper, sent in by a thoughtful reader. I am eternally grateful to that anonymous cook because I have made this wonderful cake literally dozens of times. It keeps remarkably well for a week or more when properly stored in an air-tight container.

The excellent brown sugar frosting does double duty as a candy. Just add 1/2 cup of chopped nuts, pour into a shallow, buttered pan, and cut into squares when cool.

1	cup (2 sticks) unsalted butter
2	cups superfine sugar
2	cups rich, good-quality applesauce
3	cups flour
1	teaspoon cinnamon
1	teaspoon nutmeg
1/2	teaspoon mace
1 3/4	teaspoons baking soda
1	cup pecans, coarsely chopped
1	cup raisins
1	teaspoon vanilla

Brown Sugar Frosting
2	cups light brown sugar
6	tablespoons heavy cream
1/4	cup (1/2 stick) unsalted butter
1	teaspoon vanilla
1	cup confectioners' sugar

Preheat oven to 325 degrees. Grease a 9-inch tube pan; then cut a piece of waxed paper to fit in the bottom and grease it lightly. Dust the whole pan lightly with flour, shaking out the excess.

Cream butter and sugar together thoroughly, then fold in the applesauce. This will not mix completely, so don't be alarmed.

Sift together the flour, spices, and baking soda. Remove 1/4 cup to dredge the nuts and raisins in (together). Fold the flour mixture into the butter/sugar mixture, then add the vanilla and last the nut/raisin mixture.

Pour into the prepared pan and bake in a

preheated oven for 1 1/2 hours, or until done. Allow to cool in the pan, then invert to remove.

Place all the ingredients for the frosting except the vanilla and confectioners' sugar into a pan and bring slowly to a rolling boil, stirring all the while. Remove from the heat and stir in the vanilla and then the confectioners' sugar. Pour onto the top of the spice cake and allow to run down the outer sides. This tends to set rather quickly so don't try to control the flow—the frosting will look most appetizing if allowed to flow naturally.

Serves 12

Lord Baltimore Cake

This cake can be made in either 2 or 3 layers. If you do it in 3, use pans with removable bottoms as the layers will be thin and sometimes rather reluctant to come out.

2 1/2	cups cake flour
4	teaspoons baking powder
12	tablespoons (1 1/2 sticks) unsalted butter
1 1/2	cups sugar
8	egg yolks
3/4	cup milk
1/2	teaspoon vanilla

Frosting
2 1/2	cups sugar
3/4	cup water
3	egg whites
1/2	teaspoon cream of tartar
3/4	teaspoon orange juice
3	teaspoons lemon juice
18	candied cherries, cut into quarters
3/4	cup macaroons, crumbled
3/4	cup pecans, coarsely chopped
3/4	cup blanched almonds, coarsely chopped

Preheat oven to 350 degrees. Grease 2 or 3 9-inch cake pans and dust lightly with flour, shaking out the excess.

Sift the flour and baking powder together twice and set aside. Cream butter and sugar together thoroughly. Add egg yolks all at one time and beat well. Add flour alternately with milk and beat well after each addition. Stir in vanilla.

Pour into the prepared pans and bake 25 minutes for a double-layer cake, slightly less for a triple-layer one. Remove from oven and allow to cool in the pans a few minutes. Run a knife around the edges and invert onto a cooling rack. Rap the pan gently so that cake will come out. If it doesn't, allow to cool 10 minutes or so longer. Try again.

To make frosting, dissolve sugar in the water and bring to a boil. Continue until syrup spins a thread (238 degrees on a candy thermometer). Beat egg whites stiffly and add the cream of tartar (have these ready to go when the syrup is ready to be added). Continue beating while you add the syrup in a steady stream. Add lemon and orange juice and mix. Set aside ½ the icing, and pour the other ½ in with the remaining ingredients. Use the first ½ of the icing to frost between the 3 layers of the cake, securing them with toothpicks. Frost the top and sides of the cake with the other batch.

Serves 12

Meringue Nut Cookies

This is another recipe that was given to me by my friend and fellow food enthusiast, Jean Thackery. It makes about 3 dozen cookies that never last very long and give real meaning to the term "meltingly good." Try them with the homemade Strawberry Ice Cream on page 113.

3	egg whites
⅛	teaspoon salt
½	teaspoon cream of tartar
¾	cup sugar
1½	to 2 cups pecans or walnuts, coarsely chopped, or an equal amount of hazelnuts left whole

Preheat oven to 200 degrees. Lightly butter and flour (barely) a sheet of waxed paper and place it on a cookie sheet.

Beat egg whites, and when they are foamy add salt and cream of tartar. Beat until stiff, then stir in the sugar gradually. Add the nuts and fold in carefully.

Drop batter onto the waxed paper-lined cookie sheet. Since these cookies do not rise or spread they can be placed fairly close together, but do not let them touch.

Bake for 1 hour or 1 hour and 15 minutes. Remove and allow to cool. Carefully peel them off the paper.

Makes 36 cookies

Strawberry Shortcake

This recipe calls for a warm, buttered, slightly sweet biscuit instead of the usual sponge cake. The fact that it must be served warm—as well as its generous size—disqualifies it as a dessert I would serve at the end of a meal, but it makes a perfect candidate for an afternoon surprise.

4	cups hulled and sliced strawberries
1	tablespoon sugar, or to taste
1	pint whipping cream
½	teaspoon vanilla
2	cups flour
2½	teaspoons baking powder
1	teaspoon salt
6	tablespoons (¾ stick) chilled unsalted butter
¾	cup milk
	Whole berries for garnish and extra butter for biscuits

Place hulled and sliced berries in a bowl and mash about a quarter of them. Add sugar to taste. Refrigerate. Whip cream and add the vanilla (also sugar if you like; I don't). Refrigerate.

When ready to serve, preheat the oven to 450 degrees. Mix the dry ingredients and then cut in the chilled butter (sliced into a dozen pieces) with a pastry blender or two knives. When the mixture resembles coarse cornmeal, add the milk all at once and mix well, and quickly. Turn out onto a floured board and knead briefly.

Roll out dough to ½ inch thickness, cut into approximately eight 3-inch rounds, place on an ungreased cookie sheet, and brush the tops with milk. You may also sprinkle them with sugar. Bake 12 to 15 minutes.

Assemble dessert by splitting the still hot biscuits and putting them on individual plates. Spread both halves lightly with sweet butter. When this has melted, add berries and a topping of whipped cream to the bottom half. Cover with the other half. Add more whipped cream and berries. Garnish with a whole berry or two.

Serves 6

Note: Leftover biscuits are good buttered and sprinkled with cinnamon and sugar, then toasted.

During the summer, whenever the weather cooperates, do as a friend of mine does and set up everything for dinner on the lawn. A decorative old quilt thrown over the table is a charming touch.

MORE

DINNERS

More Dinners

Because dinners are usually the most important meal of the day, I have included more menus for them than for lunches. And because they tend to be more special, it is a nice time to include extra guests. Also, if you had to make a "serious" lunch and an important dinner in one day, not much time would be left for you to have for yourself or to enjoy your houseguests. Besides, as is obvious from "More Lunches" and "No-Work Lunches," the midday meal is a lot easier to put together because it usually is composed of staples and foods that don't need too much cooking.

You'll notice the menus that follow often include an extra vegetable or condiment and/or biscuits or rolls. They are there because I enjoy doing them, and I think they add a bit of zip to a meal; but if you are too harried, these are elements that can be jettisoned without upsetting the overall plan. Rolls and breads can be purchased ready-made if you don't want to spend the time making them from scratch. Vegetables can be combined or where there is more than one, one of them can be eliminated. They could also be replaced altogether by a simple salad.

Like everything else in the book, these menus reflect personal preferences and are foods that I especially like served together. Although I don't feel there is anything definitive about them, I would like to suggest you try them as they are a few times before you substitute your personal favorites for mine. You might be missing a treat if you don't. I know I have been delighted more than once by dining on foods that I thought I didn't particularly like because of the combinations in which I found them.

I have said it elsewhere, but I think it bears repeating: Do prepare everything that you possibly can before guests arrive. I mean this literally. I go so far as to measure out ingredients and have them ready to assemble. I get the pans out that I'll be using and oil them if necessary. It is amazing how your timing can be disrupted if you don't know exactly where something is or, worse still, if you discover that you need some ingredient you thought you had, but don't. Of course, always set up the coffee and the coffee service along with the dessert service and salad service, if you are having a salad. Get the fire ready, and make sure you have enough ice and mixers. With all this done in advance, you will then have time to relax and read the paper.

The only problem in all of this for me is that I start having so much fun in the living room, it is sometimes hard to get myself back into the kitchen. I haven't solved that one yet.

Brandy custard topped with a generous grind of nutmeg.

Crispy okra and corn fritters.

In the Yard

Dining in the backyard can be great fun if the spirit is right. Hang the radio in the trees, and if you don't have exactly the right kind of outdoor furniture for the occasion, don't worry. Move the dining room table and chairs outside and pretend it is a Swedish movie.

MENU
(for 6 to 8)

Barbecued Veal
Warm String Bean and New Potato Salad
Okra-Corn Fritters
Brandy Custard with Fresh Berries
Wine
Coffee

Start this dinner right after lunch and then you can forget about it. Since the veal must marinate for 4 or 5 hours, longer if you like, just be sure you allow enough time. The bean and potato salad is served warm or at room temperature, and since the meat can rest for about 30 minutes after it cooks, you have plenty of leeway. The fritters must be done last so they will be hot. Dessert is finished and put aside in the afternoon.

Barbecued veal with string beans and new potatoes.

In the Yard

Barbecued Veal

Veal can be very expensive, so I use a shoulder/neck cut or the leg in this recipe, since the veal is doused with a strong marinade. Sometimes veal can be found in your market rolled. Simply untie it and remove any connective gristle or tissue. Failing that, your butcher can prepare it for you. It is not always available, so call in advance.

Vegetable Marinade

1	large onion
3	large cloves garlic
1	green pepper
2	bunches green onions, some top included
6	sprigs parsley
1/2	cup peanut oil
1/2	cup tomato sauce
1/2	cup wine vinegar
1/4	cup Worcestershire sauce
1/4	cup honey
1	teaspoon salt
1/4	teaspoon freshly ground black pepper
1/8	teaspoon Tabasco sauce
2	heaping teaspoons small capers
1	3½- to 4-pound boned and butterflied shoulder or leg of veal

Put onion, garlic, green pepper, green onions, and parsley, all of which have been washed and cleaned and then cut into large pieces, into a food processor fitted with a metal blade. Switching off and on and scraping down sides, process to medium-size bits.

Heat oil in a large skillet and, when hot, add contents of food processor bowl. Simmer for 5 minutes over medium heat. Add other ingredients except veal and continue to simmer for 20 minutes. Taste for seasoning and allow to cool.

Put meat into a crockery bowl and pack the cooled marinade over it (this marinade has lots of vegetables in it). Cover and refrigerate for 4 or 5 hours, turning it once or twice.

About an hour before you are ready to start the meat cooking, take it from the refrigerator so that it will be room temperature. Prepare coals for barbecue. When they are white, put the meat on the grill. Also turn oven on to preheat to 375 degrees. Grill meat for 15 minutes per side.

In the meantime, heat the barbecue marinade (you may use a bit of it to baste the meat while it is cooking if you like, but it is not really necessary). After the ½ hour grilling time, put veal into a deep skillet with a close-fitting lid and pour heated sauce over it. Cover and bake for 1 to 1½ hours. Test for tenderness after an hour; continue cooking for the additional ½ hour if it seems tough. When it is done, remove from the oven and keep warm (lightly covered) until time to serve. It can sit this way for a half hour. Pour a bit of the sauce over each serving and serve the rest on the side.

Note: I use this method of cooking because veal dries out too much if cooked entirely over the coals.

Serves 6–8

Warm String Bean and New Potato Salad

Some people cook these vegetables separately when serving them this way, but I just dump them all in a pot together. I like the flavor the cooking juice adds to the potatoes.

2	pounds string beans, snapped into several pieces, ends removed
2	pounds small red new potatoes, scrubbed
2	large onions, chopped coarsely
1	1-inch piece salt pork
	Salt and freshly ground black pepper to taste

Vinaigrette Dressing

2	tablespoons lemon juice (fresh only), more to taste
3	tablespoons safflower oil
2	tablespoons olive oil
1	teaspoon salt, or to taste
1	generous teaspoon powdered mustard
	Scant 1/4 teaspoon black pepper
	Chopped parsley (optional)

Put beans and potatoes in a saucepan. Cover with water and add the onions, salt pork, and salt and pepper. Simmer for 30 to 40 minutes. The beans should be very tender. They can cool a bit in the liquid. When ready to serve, if they have gotten completely cold, bring the liquid back to a boil and then turn off the heat. Allow vegetables to sit in it while you whisk together all the ingredients for the dressing.

Drain the vegetables, discarding the cooking liquid or keeping it for soup. Put in a serving bowl and toss with the dressing. Chopped parsley may be added. Correct seasoning if necessary.

Serves 6–8

Okra-Corn Fritters

I know not all people share my enthusiasm for okra. If you are one of them, you can make plain corn fritters instead of these. Just replace the okra with an equal quantity of corn.

	Oil for frying
2	eggs, separated
1/2	cup milk
1 1/3	cups sifted white cornmeal
2	teaspoons baking powder
3/4	teaspoon salt
	Dash of pepper
1/2	cup fresh raw corn, cut from the cob with scrapings
2	tablespoons minced parsley
1/2	cup okra, in 1/2-inch rings, steamed for 2 to 3 minutes

Put oil in a skillet to a depth of 2 inches. Heat to 350 degrees.

Beat egg yolks, then add milk and mix. Sift together cornmeal, baking powder, salt, and pepper. Add to the yolk mixture. Mix quickly. Do not overmix.

Have ready the raw corn, parsley, and steamed okra. Combine with the batter. Beat egg whites until stiff, heap on top, and carefully fold in.

Drop batter by tablespoons into the heated oil. Turn once if necessary. When golden, about 3 to 4 minutes, remove with a slotted spoon and allow to drain on paper towels. Serve immediately.

Note: A word of caution about corn fritters: If a large quantity of corn is used and if it is very mature, it will sometimes spatter a bit, so you should have a "spatter shield" or large lightweight lid handy just in case. You will be able to tell if you are going to have this nuisance after cooking the first batch.

Makes 16 fritters

Brandy Custard with Fresh Berries

This recipe came to me from a friend who had gotten it from her grandmother. I've tried many old recipes and have discovered that a large number of the desserts are sweeter than similar ones popular today. For that reason, I have reduced the amount of sugar called for in the original.

1	pint whole milk
2	eggs, separated
1/2	to 3/4 cup sugar
2	tablespoons flour
1	tablespoon brandy
	Grated nutmeg
	Fresh raspberries or other berries

Let milk come to boil in a double boiler. Beat egg yolks well and mix with half the sugar and the flour. Stir into the hot milk. Continue to stir until thickened. Strain immediately.

Beat egg whites until very stiff and add the remaining sugar. Beat long enough to incorporate. Stir into the custard mixture. Add 1 tablespoon or more brandy, to taste, and pour into individual custard pots. Top with grated nutmeg. Fresh berries can be sprinkled on top or served on the side. This custard may be chilled slightly, but should not be refrigerated.

Serves 6–8

An old porch like this, just off the kitchen, is a delightful spot for dining—and convenient, too.

On the
Porch

On the Porch

MENU
(for 6)

Double-Crust Chicken and Dumpling Pie
Steamed Lima Beans with Brown Butter
Wilted Red Onion and Pickled Beet Salad
Peppered Peaches
Peppermint Ice Milk
Shortbread
Wine
Coffee

This Chicken and Dumpling Pie with its double crust is interesting and sounds complicated, but it isn't really. You just have to understand what you are doing. I have purposely made the balance of the meal as uncomplicated as possible so that you can devote all of your attention to the pie when you make it the first time. The second time it will be a breeze.

Double-Crust Chicken and Dumpling Pie

You will need a deep baking dish that has a capacity of approximately 5 quarts and is about the size of a small roasting pan. As a matter of fact, if all else fails, you can use a roasting pan; it just won't make as nice a presentation. Also handy, but not absolutely necessary, are a pastry wheel and a funnel with a handle.

In this pie, the dumplings and double top crusts are all made from the same dough, which makes the texture of the dish more interesting. For those of you who are accustomed to small square or round dumplings, these are different; they are made in long strips.

Dumplings and Crust

5	cups flour
9	teaspoons baking powder
1/2	teaspoon baking soda
1	teaspoon salt
1	cup (2 sticks) chilled unsalted butter, cut into 16 pieces
2	cups buttermilk
6	cups hot chicken stock
3 1/2	to 4 pounds mixed chicken breasts and thighs, skin removed, the breast halves cut in two
	Salt and pepper
1 1/2	cups finely chopped celery
1/2	cup finely chopped red onion

Preheat oven to 450 degrees. Lightly grease the pan and set aside.

Sift all the dry ingredients for the dumplings and crust into a large bowl. Cut in the butter with two knives or a pastry blender. Butter pieces should be the size of large peas when you finish the cutting in. Stir in the buttermilk and make a ball of dough. Turn it onto a floured surface and knead it for just a few minutes. Divide it into 2 equal parts. One ball will be used to line pan and make dumplings, the other for the double crust. Dust each with a little flour and cover with a tea towel.

To assemble the dish, put the chicken stock on to heat and roll out half of one of the balls of dough to about 1/4-inch thickness. With a pastry wheel, cut a long strip or two to fit around the sides of the pan, leaving the bottom unlined. You may want to press the dough along the top rim of the pan to hold it in place. Neatness is not important here, as this is temporary. Set aside any leftover rolled-out dough. Using half the chicken pieces, make a single layer in the bottom of the pan. Sprinkle with salt and pepper and half the celery and onion.

To make dumplings, roll out the other half ball of dough to 1/4-inch thickness. Cut it into strips 1 inch wide. Lay half of them lengthwise across the chicken parts in the pan. Gently place the remainder of the chicken on top of the strips of dough and sprinkle with salt and pepper and vegetables as before. Cover with remaining strips of dough, also as before.

To make the top crusts, divide the second ball of dough into 2 parts. Roll out one part to the size of the top of the pan. (If you like, cut out a paper pattern the size of the top of the pan before you start, to use as a guide.) Lay dough, which will be rather thin and elastic, over chicken and dumplings, covering the entire top. If you are apprehensive about picking up this large sheet of dough, you may cut it into 2 or 4 pieces and reassemble on the pie. The crust will be slightly below the top edge of the pan, to allow for it to float up when the liquid is added. To join the top to the sides, push the side strips so that they fall over onto the top crust. They will melt together slightly while baking.

Make a hole in the center of the top crust and pour in the 6 cups of boiling stock. This is where the funnel helps. This is also when the top crust will float up. Bake for 25 minutes in the preheated oven, until golden brown. About 5 minutes before this cooking time is up, melt 3 tablespoons butter or margarine.

To make the final crust, roll out the remaining piece of dough to the size of the top of the pan. Take pie from the oven and, using half the melted butter, paint the cooked crust with a pastry brush. Place the uncooked second crust over the top of the first, making sure it covers completely. Trim off any dough that may be hanging over. Carefully paint this last crust with the remaining shortening. Return to the oven, turn it down to 250 degrees, and cook an additional 65 minutes. The total cooking time is 1½ hours.

To serve, cut a piece of the top (and side) crust and place on the plate first, then spoon out chicken and dumplings over it. This is a juicy pie, so plan to have your salad on a separate plate.

Note: I discovered once, while making this, that the dough can be made the day before, divided into 2 parts, and refrigerated tightly wrapped in plastic wrap. If you do this, take it out of the refrigerator 30 minutes or so before you intend to use it. Because of the baking time, this pie should be in the oven when your guests arrive. If you want to eat at 9:30 it should be in by 7:30.

Serves 6–8

Steamed Lima Beans with Brown Butter

Lima beans are the one vegetable that I use frozen, because they taste almost as good as fresh and save a lot of time. Steam two 10-ounce packages according to the directions. Carefully brown butter to nut color in a skillet and pour over all just before serving.

Peaches dressed with lemon juice and cayenne pepper.

Lima beans in brown butter.

Pickled beet and wilted red onion salad.

Double-crust chicken and dumpling pie—an interesting version of the old classic.

Homemade peppermint ice milk and old-fashioned shortbread squares.

Wilted Red Onions and Pickled Beet Salad

These onions make delicious sandwiches or a topping for tomatoes. Like the beets, they keep well in the refrigerator. To serve, put a portion of beets and onions on each individual salad plate.

Wilted Onions
1½   pounds red onions, peeled and sliced thin
½   cup safflower oil
½   cup white vinegar
½   cup water
½   teaspoon pepper
2   teaspoons salt
1   tablespoon sugar
3   or 4 drops Tabasco sauce

Put onions in a crockery bowl. Mix all other ingredients together in a saucepan and bring to a boil. Pour over the onions. When cool, cover and refrigerate overnight.

Pickled Beets
1½   cups white vinegar
½   cup sugar
½   teaspoon salt
1   teaspoon whole allspice
1½   cups water
9   unpeeled medium-size beets, roots and tops removed, cut into 4 wedges (about 2½ cups)
6   green onions, including some of the green, cut into ½-inch lengths (about ½ cup)
2   sprigs fresh tarragon, each about 3 inches long, or 1 teaspoon dried

Combine vinegar, sugar, salt, allspice, and water in a medium-size saucepan. Simmer over moderate heat (if using dry tarragon, add it now). Reduce heat and simmer 10 minutes. Add beets, cover, and cook over moderate heat 10 to 15 minutes, or until beets are tender. Cool beets in cooking liquid for about 30 minutes and skin them.

Transfer beets and liquid to a jar or bowl. Add the green onions and fresh tarragon. Cover with cheesecloth and let stand overnight. Next day, remove cheesecloth and refrigerate, covered.

Serves 6, with leftovers

Peppered Peaches

This dish is East Indian in origin and has a nice tang that goes well with poultry and meat dishes.

6   large peaches, peeled, pitted, and halved
3   tablespoons fresh lemon juice
2   tablespoons sugar
1   teaspoon salt
    Black pepper and cayenne pepper

To peel peaches, dip in boiling water for 6 seconds. Skins should then slip off easily. Put peach halves in a single layer on a plate and coat with lemon juice. Sprinkle sugar and salt over all. Add black pepper and cayenne pepper sparingly. After you have made this once, you can increase the amounts of peppers to suit your taste.

This dish can be prepared up to 3 hours in advance. Don't refrigerate. The lemon juice keeps the peaches from discoloring.

Serves 6

Peppermint Ice Milk

To make rich ice cream, use basic ice milk recipe below but substitute 1 cup half-and-half for the evaporated skim milk and 1 cup whole milk for the 1 cup low-fat milk. Add 6 crushed peppermint canes or round candies before freezing.

6   tablespoons sugar
½   teaspoon flour
1   pinch of salt
1   cup evaporated skim milk
1   egg, beaten
1   teaspoon vanilla
1   cup low-fat milk

Mix sugar, flour, and salt in the top of a double boiler. Stir in skim milk. Cook over boiling water for 5 minutes, stirring all the while. Cover and cook for 10 minutes more. Turn off heat. Spoon a little of the hot milk mixture into the beaten egg and then return all to the double boiler. This time cook over hot, not boiling, water, stirring constantly, for about 5 minutes, or until mixture begins to coat spoon. Strain and chill.

Add vanilla and whole milk. Put into an automatic ice cream freezer.

Makes 1½ pints

Shortbread

This is a very old recipe. Like many such, it is wonderfully simple. The end product improves with age. You will note that the recipe calls for granulated sugar rather than confectioner's sugar; this contributes to its crunchy texture.

- ½ cup (1 stick) unsalted butter
- ½ cup sugar
- 2 cups flour

Preheat oven to 300 degrees.

Mix all the ingredients together with your hands until dough resembles coarse meal. The theory is that the warmth of your hands softens the butter and makes the shortbread crispy.

Pat the mixture into an ungreased 9 × 9-inch pan. Pierce the dough every 2 inches with a fork. Bake for 40 minutes, or until slightly brown. Cut into squares while still warm.

Makes 16 squares

Butter Pecan Cookies*

These delicious and easy-to-make cookies are another excellent accompaniment to the ice cream. They were the only thing my mother ever learned to cook—one of those eccentric choices that probably are just accidents. She used to make them and send them to me regularly when I was away at school and later when I was in the army.

- ¾ cup (1½ sticks) unsalted butter
- 1 cup pecans, grated
- 4 tablespoons powdered sugar
- 1 tablespoon ice water
- 2 cups flour
- 2 teaspoons vanilla
  Additional powdered sugar

Preheat oven to 325 degrees.

Cream together butter and sugar. Mix in the flour and pecans. Add ice water and mix. Add vanilla and mix.

Roll into balls or crescents and place on 1 (or 2) ungreased cookie sheets. Bake 20 minutes or until cookies just begin to brown. Roll them in the additional powdered sugar while still warm.

Note: Two standard-size cookie sheets usually won't fit on one shelf of a regular oven, so it is a good idea to buy a slightly smaller one to be used when you want to bake with two pans at the same time.

Makes 5 dozen

*Alternate to Shortbread recipe

Under the Pines

Under the Pines

MENU
(for 6)

*Lovage-and-Apple-Stuffed Roast Chicken
with Pan Gravy*

Grits Soufflé

Beet and Carrot Purée

Flaky Biscuits with Parsley Butter

*Grapefruit Sherbet with
Candied Grapefruit Rind*

Wine

Coffee

Lovage is an herb that is very hardy in the garden but for some reason has never become as popular as other common herbs. Growing, it looks like celery leaves and even has a stronger celerylike taste, accompanied by a slightly resinous aftertaste that is both pleasant and unexpected. If you can't find it, use celery tops. If you have a garden, plant it.

Everything in this menu except the soufflé will hold well for varying lengths of time. The chicken and gravy can finish an hour before serving, with the gravy just needing a little warming up. The beets reheat easily. If you have two ovens, time the biscuits and soufflé to come out together. If not, the biscuits can be baked just before the soufflé goes in, and buttered to be reheated in with the soufflé for the last few minutes of its cooking time.

Lovage-and-Apple-Stuffed Roast Chicken with Pan Gravy

I have come to like chicken served warm rather than hot, as Europeans seem to prefer it. The flavor when served with hot gravy seems to be more intense.

2	2½-pound whole chickens
1	teaspoon salt
¼	teaspoon freshly ground black pepper
1	cup (2 sticks) unsalted butter, softened
1	large cooking apple, peeled and cored
1	handful lovage

Gravy

1	tablespoon butter, softened
2	tablespoons flour
1	cup chicken stock, heated
1	tablespoon chopped chives (optional)

Preheat oven to 425 degrees.

Prepare chickens by washing them thoroughly and patting dry inside and out. Mix salt and pepper into the softened butter. Peel and core the apple and chop into ½-inch pieces. Pull stems out of a handful of lovage and tear apart. Put a bit of the seasoned butter in each chicken cavity. Then alternate the seasoned butter, lovage, and apples until cavities are filled. Close cavities.

Place both chickens, breast up, on rack in a roasting pan. Smear balance of the salt/pepper/ butter mixture on the outside skin. Put in preheated oven and bake for approximately 1 hour and 15 minutes, basting with more butter, or accumulated pan juices, every 15 minutes. Test for doneness by pulling leg away from body. If it moves easily and the juice seems clear, it is done. Remove chicken to warm platter. Cover and let stand.

You can make the gravy at this point by combining soft butter and flour and mashing them together with a fork to make a paste. Have ready 1 cup hot chicken stock. Pour off chicken fat from pan and add stock. Swirl it around to loosen any browned bits stuck to the bottom of the pan. These are what give the gravy added flavor. Thicken with butter-flour mixture. Correct seasoning if necessary. A tablespoon of chopped chives can be added just before serving. Simmer very carefully for 15 minutes. If gravy becomes too thick, add a little more stock.

Serves 6

Grits Soufflé

I like the subtle change of flavor that happens when grits are made into a soufflé. This soufflé is really very easy to do. The only important thing is timing. Make sure to have everything else ready to serve when you take the soufflé out of the oven. If you are delayed a bit, the dish will still taste good, but it will sink somewhat.

1	cup milk
1	cup water
2	teaspoons salt
1/2	cup white hominy grits (not instant or quick-cooking kind)
5	tablespoons unsalted butter
1/4	teaspoon black pepper
3	egg yolks
5	ounces sharp Cheddar cheese, grated
9	egg whites
1/4	teaspoon cream of tartar

Preheat oven to 450 degrees. Butter a 2-quart soufflé dish and set aside.

Combine milk, water, and salt in a saucepan and bring to a boil. Add grits, stirring. Continue to cook for about 5 minutes, or until the mixture thickens. Remove from heat and add the butter and pepper. Mix. Add egg yolks and mix. Add 4 ounces of Cheddar cheese and mix. Set aside.

Beat egg whites until stiff. Beat in cream of tartar. Heap a third of the egg whites onto grits and fold in with rubber spatula. It is best to use a rolling motion, over and under, when mixing egg whites into a batter. Fold in the rest of the whites.

Pour mixture into buttered dish and sprinkle with remaining cheese. Put on top of a cookie sheet on middle shelf in oven. Bake for 35 minutes, until golden and puffed.

Note: If you happen to misjudge the cooking time and the soufflé is not cooked enough, don't worry. It will be creamier in the center and taste equally as good, so you can't lose.

Serves 6

Creamed Corn Pudding*

The Grits Soufflé in this menu is the one dish that should be eaten as soon as you take it from the oven. If you feel this would make timing a little too tight to suit you, here is an alternate recipe for a corn custard that, although it should be eaten hot, gives you somewhat more flexibility. If you decide on substituting it, the important element in the recipe is the fresh corn base. Because fresh corn varies in water content from year to year, it is almost impossible to say exactly the number of ears you will require. It may be anywhere from 6 to 8, or even more if they are small or dry. I would rather have a bit more (you can eat any leftover corn, as is, with a dab of butter).

This is one of those old family recipes. I think you will love it.

2 1/2	cups fresh corn, cut from the cob
1	cup light cream or evaporated skimmed milk
1	tablespoon sugar
1 1/2	teaspoons salt
1/4	teaspoon white pepper
3	tablespoons butter, melted
5	eggs, well beaten
3	cups milk
1	tablespoon cornstarch
1	tablespoon cold water

Preheat oven to 350 degrees. Generously butter a shallow 2-quart baking dish.

Cut corn from the cob and scrape out the juice, using the back of the knife blade. You should have about 2 1/2 cups pulp and juice. Place this in the top of a double boiler along with the light cream or evaporated skimmed milk. Slowly cook for 10 to 20 minutes to reduce it slightly. Stir often to prevent sticking. This should produce a thickened creamy mixture. If it starts to dry out, add more cream, or if it is too liquid, cook a little longer.

Measure out 2 1/2 cups of this corn mixture to use in the custard. If you don't have quite enough to make the measure, stir in a few more tablespoons of cream. This may be set aside now for 30 minutes or so if your timing is off. It should cool down a bit before you use it anyway.

Combine corn mixture with the sugar, salt, pepper, butter, eggs, and milk. Dissolve cornstarch in the water and add. Pour into the prepared baking dish and bake for about 1 hour or until custard is firm.

Serves 6 to 8

*Alternate to Grits Soufflé recipe

Dining in a sheltered spot under the trees is one of the real pleasures of summer.

Small roast chickens stuffed with a mixture of lovage and apple.

This grits soufflé is more stable than most and should hold its shape long enough for your guests to admire.

Flaky biscuits.

Grapefruit sherbet with candied grapefruit rind.

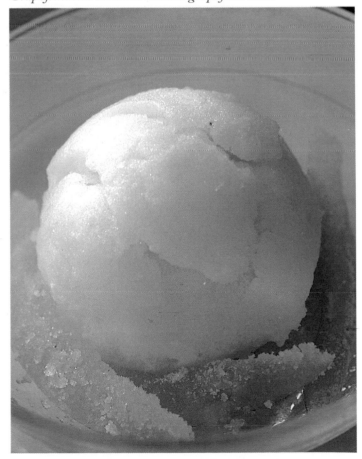

Beet and Carrot Purée

I think the touch of carrot here is a pleasant addition to this purée.

1¾ pounds fresh beets with tops and root end removed
½ pound carrots, scraped and cut into 1-inch pieces
¼ cup (½ stick) unsalted butter
½ teaspoon salt
1 teaspoon lemon juice
1 tablespoon sugar

Cover beets with water and cook until very tender. This can take up to 1 hour if beets are large. At the same time, cook carrots ½ hour, or until tender. Drain. When beets are tender, remove from heat and the skin will slip off. If beets are large, cut into pieces. Put into a food processor along with the carrots. Process a few seconds and scrape the bowl down. Add all the other ingredients and process until you have a smooth purée. Taste and correct the seasoning, adding more sugar or salt if necessary. Keep warm. If it is to be reheated, do so in the top of a double boiler.

Serves 6

Flaky Biscuits with Parsley Butter

Increasing the butter in biscuits makes them tenderer and flakier as well as more flavorful.

2 cups sifted flour
¼ teaspoon salt
3 teaspoons baking powder
6 tablespoons (¾ stick) cold unsalted butter (in 6 pieces)
⅔ cup milk

Preheat oven to 450 degrees.

Sift dry ingredients together into a bowl. Cut in the butter with two knives or a pastry blender. The butter should be the size of small peas. Add the milk and mix quickly. Turn out onto a floured surface and roll with a floured pin or flatten with the heel of your hand to about ⅜-inch thickness. Cut with a biscuit cutter or a water glass. Set apart on a heavy cookie sheet and paint the top of each with a little milk. You can do this with your finger. Bake for 10 minutes or more, until golden.

Serve with parsley butter.

Makes about 1½ dozen biscuits

Parsley Butter

The hint of parsley here goes well with the chicken and other dishes in this meal. Herbed butters should only be made with the freshest of herbs because it is this freshness that gives them their distinctiveness. In place of parsley you could use chives or, less successfully, dill. Any other herb would probably compete too much with the lovage stuffing.

½ cup (1 stick) unsalted butter, softened
1 tablespoon parsley, finely chopped

Mash the parsley into the butter and scrape it into a small crock to serve.

Grapefruit Sherbet with Candied Grapefruit Rind

The light, fresh taste of the grapefruit, with the surprise of its crystallized rind, makes a refreshing finish to a meal.

½	to 1 grapefruit, unpeeled, cut into ½-inch pieces (1½ cups)
½	cup superfine sugar
1½	cups water
2	tablespoons fresh grapefruit juice
2	teaspoons lemon juice
1	egg white, beaten into soft peaks
2	jiggers vodka

Put grapefruit in a small saucepan with only enough water to cover and boil slowly until tender (5 to 10 minutes). Drain, discarding the water. Combine grapefruit with 3 tablespoons of sugar. Put in food processor fitted with a metal blade and mix until grapefruit is puréed.

In a small saucepan combine remaining sugar and water. Heat over slow flame until sugar dissolves. Remove and allow to cool. Put this sugar syrup in freezer for 10 to 15 minutes.

Put grapefruit purée in another saucepan and simmer slowly until thick, 15 to 20 minutes. Keep an eye on it and don't let it scorch. Remove from heat and stir in grapefruit juice. Combine chilled syrup, grapefruit purée, and lemon juice. Just before freezing, add beaten egg whites and stir in vodka. Put in automatic ice cream freezer. Serve with pieces of Candied Grapefruit Rind.

Makes 8 servings

Candied Grapefruit Rind

Gael Greene gave me the recipe for these delicious little strips of rind. They could, of course, be eaten by themselves but are a nice addition to the sherbet here.

1	large grapefruit
	Equal amounts of water and granulated sugar
	Granulated sugar for coating

With a knife, remove peel from grapefruit in thick slices, leaving some of the fruit on the rind. Cover with cold water in a pot and bring to a boil and boil 10 minutes. Drain. Cover again with cold water and repeat 2 more times. Drain. Cover with a mixture of equal amounts of cold water and sugar. The quantity will vary according to the amount of grapefruit peel you have. Bring to a boil. Boil 10 minutes. Drain. Let dry slightly until cool. Cut into long strips and press into granulated sugar to coat the rind.

The ingredients for a simple coleslaw.

Shelled green peas ready for steaming.

On the Deck

Old-fashioned fish fries were always a part of summer for me when I was growing up. Everything was served outside on a long table. Sometimes, the fish was even fried outdoors. I don't think you have to go that far, but when I saw this long table on a friend's deck, it reminded me of those dinners.

Alternate slices of lemon and tomato on a platter.

Homemade strawberry ice cream with strawberry purée.

On the Deck

MENU
(for 6)

Fried Fish Fillets
Tartar Sauce
Tomatoes with Lemon Slices
Cole Slaw
Steamed Green Peas
Strawberry Ice Cream with Strawberry Purée
Wine and Beer
Coffee

I've found that even people who profess not to be fish fanciers enjoy this meal.

Everything should be prepared and ready before you start frying the fish. Also remember a few minutes are needed for the shortening to heat. Start the fish just after the peas finish steaming. Use two pans so it will all go quickly.

Fried Fish Fillets

Any kind of fish can be prepared in this manner, but my favorite is a fillet of something mild like bass or snapper.

3   pounds fresh fish fillets, washed
Milk to cover
Cornmeal to coat
Salt and pepper to taste
Oil for frying

About 30 minutes before you want to start frying, put the fillets in a shallow bowl and cover with milk. Refrigerate.

Put two large skillets on to heat, each with about an inch of oil in it. Meanwhile, sprinkle a

generous amount of yellow cornmeal on a sheet of waxed paper. Have this right next to the stove. Drain the milk off the fish, pat fish dry, and dredge in the cornmeal, making sure it is well coated. Salt and pepper if you like. Fry in the hot oil until golden. Try to turn only once. Drain on absorbent paper and keep warm. Serve with homemade Tartar Sauce.

Note: This oil can be used to fry fish again (but nothing else). Strain it into a bottle and keep refrigerated.

Serves 6

Tartar Sauce

There are a large number of ingredients in this sauce because I like it that way, but it can also be made with just mayonnaise, pickles, and chives.

1   cup homemade mayonnaise (page 153)
1   tablespoon parsley, chopped fine
1   tablespoon chives, chopped fine
1   tablespoon small capers
2   tablespoons sweet pickles, chopped fine
1   large green onion, some top, chopped fine
    Scant 1/4 teaspoon Dijon mustard
3   or 4 grinds fresh black pepper
    Salt to taste
    Chopped fresh dill

Mix all the ingredients except dill and refrigerate until ready to use. Sprinkle dill generously over the Tartar Sauce before serving.

Makes 1 generous cup sauce

Tomatoes with Lemon Slices

I serve the tomatoes with this meal without any dressing, as there is Tartar Sauce and a dressing on the Cole Slaw. By all means add a vinaigrette if the tomatoes don't appeal to you this way.

4   firm, ripe medium to large tomatoes
2   lemons
    Fresh chives

Peel the tomatoes by dipping them in boiling water for 5 or 6 seconds. Cut into thick slices, setting aside the uneven bottom slice and the small top slice. Slice the lemons very thinly and remove any seed parts. On a long platter, arrange the tomatoes in rows with the slices alternating with lemon rounds. Dice the set-aside uneven slices and heap along the middle or on the sides of the rows. Snip a bit of chives over the top of the dish.

Note: I dip the tomatoes a few hours before they are to be used and refrigerate them unpeeled until they are going to be served. If you dip and peel them and then let them sit in the refrigerator, they give up water and lose some of their texture and flavor.

Serves 6

Cole Slaw

Although I like my tartar sauce complicated, I like my cole slaw simple: just cabbage and red pepper with a basic mayonnaise dressing.

Mayonnaise Dressing
1   cup mayonnaise
1   tablespoon plus 1 teaspoon olive oil
2   tablespoons safflower oil
2   teaspoons sugar
1   teaspoon salt
1   generous teaspoon green peppercorn mustard
2   tablespoons balsamic vinegar
7   drops Tabasco sauce
1/2 teaspoon black pepper

5   cups cabbage, finely shredded
1   medium sweet red pepper, finely chopped

Whisk together all the ingredients for the dressing until well blended. Mix the cabbage and pepper together with a generous amount of dressing. You will probably have more dressing than you need. Refrigerate if not using right away.

Serves 6

Steamed Green Peas

This might be more peas than you need, but if any are left over, I put them into a salad the next day.

4   pounds green peas in the pod
1/4 cup (1/2 stick) unsalted butter
     Salt and pepper to taste

Shell peas, and steam in steamer basket until tender. The time will vary according to how old and how large the peas are. Toss with the butter, adding more if you like. Season with salt and pepper.

Serves 6, with leftovers

Strawberry Ice Cream with Strawberry Purée

When berries are first in season, I love to make homemade strawberry ice cream. In this case I think too much is just enough so I serve it with sweetened strawberry purée, garnished with 1 or 2 nice big ripe berries rolled in confectioners' sugar.

1   pint washed, hulled, and crushed strawberries
1   recipe for basic ice cream (see variation page 100)
1   cup strawberries, washed, hulled, and sliced, plus a few extra perfect ones for garnish
     Few drops lemon juice
     Sugar to taste
     Confectioners' sugar

Add the crushed berries to the basic ice cream mixture and put into an ice cream freezer.

Purée 1 cup sliced berries and add a few drops of lemon juice along with sugar to taste. Refrigerate until serving.

Roll the garnish berries in confectioners' sugar on a plate and serve with ice cream and purée.

Serves 6

Stuffed cabbage and leeks with chopped red onion.

Fried sweet potatoes sprinkled with cinnamon and sugar.

In the Kitchen

When fall comes, weekend activities tend to move inside. This is when a rustic old kitchen, especially one with a fireplace, can become the focal point for dining. A hearty meal of stuffed cabbage, sweet potatoes, spoonbread, and rich chocolate pie is right at home in such surroundings.

MENU
(for 8)

Pork-and-Apple-Stuffed Cabbage
Steamed Leeks with Red Onion
Fried Sweet Potato Slices
Spoon Bread
Chocolate Custard Pie
Wine
Coffee

The cabbage dish in this menu is inspired by one my grandmother used to cook. Probably it wasn't done this way, but the results are close enough. The filling, I am sure, would adapt itself to many variations of seasoning. When preparing this meal, start with the cabbage, which must steam for 2 hours. The leeks can be steamed in the same pot during the last 45 minutes of cooking time. About halfway through the spoon bread's cooking time, start frying the sweet potatoes. If they finish first, they will hold. Everything should be ready when the spoon bread comes out.

Chocolate custard pie with whipped cream.

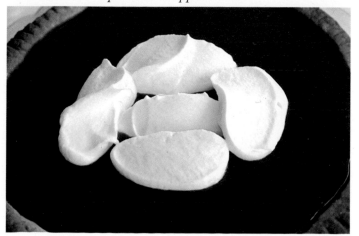

Pork-and-Apple-Stuffed Cabbage

Since there is nothing in this dish to bind it together, such as egg, it remains very light and crumbly in spite of the fact that it is packed very tightly into the cabbage head. To serve it, spoon out a bit of the meat mixture first and then cut a portion of the cabbage. Top with Tomato Sauce.

1	large head cabbage
1	pound sausage meat (I use Jones Country)
1	pound ground pork
1	pound cooked ham
4	tablespoons safflower oil
2	cups chopped onions
1	cup chopped celery
2	cups cooked rice
2	large cloves garlic, crushed or finely chopped
1	medium cooking apple
1½	teaspoons salt
1½	teaspoons thyme
¼	teaspoon cayenne pepper
½	teaspoon black pepper
4	tablespoons parsley

Tomato Sauce

2	tablespoons each clarified unsalted butter and olive oil
2	large onions, peeled and chopped coarsely
3	medium cloves garlic, peeled and cut into large chunks
1	28-ounce can tomatoes with purée (without basil)
	Salt and pepper to taste
4	or 5 fresh tarragon leaves
1	handful parsley

Peel off large outer leaves of the cabbage head. If they are in good condition, wash them and set aside to decorate the dish. Cut off the core end of the cabbage. Remove the core without disturbing the outer walls, and discard. Using a small pointed paring knife, and making short, slashing, crosshatch motions, hollow out the entire cabbage head, leaving a thin outer wall intact. This chopped cabbage can be reserved and used for another meal. Set aside.

Cook sausage meat in small batches until lightly browned and discard any fat. Do the same with the pork, then the ham. Put meats into a large mixing bowl and set aside.

Heat the oil in a skillet and cook the onions and celery until just wilted. Add these to the cooked meats along with the rice and garlic. Combine well. Peel and core the apple and chop into medium pieces. Add to rice-meat mixture and combine. Add remaining seasonings and parsley and mix well.

Place the cabbage head into a cheesecloth tube with one end knotted. Pack the stuffing into the cabbage very tightly. It may seem that you have too much stuffing, but keep packing it in and mound it very high over the top, pressing down. Tie the open end of the sock with a string so that the cabbage and stuffing are held securely in place. Put in a large steamer pot (I use a spaghetti pot with a removable perforated insert) and steam for 2 hours. It can rest here for a bit while you prepare the other elements of the dinner.

Since the cabbage mixture is crumbly, I like a thick sauce on it so that the cabbage won't be too runny. To make Tomato Sauce, put butter and oil in skillet. Add onions and sauté lightly. Add garlic and tomatoes, salt and pepper, and tarragon. Simmer about 45 minutes. Wash and stem parsley, and add to mixture. Cook about 15 minutes more. Put entire mixture into a food processor and purée.

Serves 8

Steamed Leeks with Red Onion

Steamed leeks are one of my favorite vegetables. Topped with finely chopped red onion, they are delicious.

16	medium leeks, root end and most of the green top removed
1	medium red onion, chopped fine

To clean leeks, let stand in a large quantity of cold water for 30 minutes or so. Before putting leeks in soaking water, stand on root end and, using downward motion, with a sharp knife cut halfway down the length of the stem so that the water can get in between the leaves. Pour out water, replacing it with new, pulling the leaves back slightly to make sure all the sand is out. Steam for 45 minutes.

The leeks may be served whole or cut in two, with chopped onion sprinkled over the top.

Serves 8

Fried Sweet Potato Slices

These fried sweet potatoes, like the cabbage, take me back to my childhood.

> 5 medium sweet potatoes, peeled and cut into medium-thin rounds (approximately 3/8 inch thick)
> Safflower oil for frying
> Mixed granulated sugar and cinnamon

Heat oil in large skillet and, when hot, fry potato rounds until golden. Remove to paper towels and drain. Put on serving platter and sprinkle generously with sugar-cinnamon mixture. (The preparation of this mixture is left to your own taste. You can eliminate the cinnamon if you like.) Set in a warm oven until serving.

Serves 8

Spoon Bread

There are as many different recipes for spoon bread as there are for other Southern regional favorites. This one is neither the simplest nor the most complicated, but the results are almost foolproof.

> 1½ cups white cornmeal
> 3 cups milk
> ¼ cup (½ stick) unsalted butter
> 1 teaspoon salt
> 2 teaspoons baking powder
> 4 eggs, separated
> 1 tablespoon sugar

Preheat oven to 350 degrees. Butter a 2-quart casserole and set aside.

Put cornmeal in the top of a double boiler. Heat 2 cups of milk, stir into cornmeal, and add butter. Cook 10 minutes over boiling water,

stirring all the while. This will finally make a ball. Add salt and let cool to lukewarm (about 15 minutes).

Dissolve baking powder in the remaining 1 cup milk and beat with the egg yolks. Combine with the cornmeal and sugar, mixing well. Beat egg whites until stiff and fold in with a rolling motion. Pour into the casserole and bake about 40 minutes, until puffy and brown. When serving, make sure everyone gets a bit of the brown crust or sides.

Serves 8

Chocolate Custard Pie

This produces a very liquidy pie because of its pudding filling. I like it better than a baked one because the crust can be crispier. But if this bothers you, make individual pastry tarts in a muffin pan instead of one pie. Refrigerating it for several hours before serving will also make it set more.

> 1 recipe Pie Crust (page 29)
>
> 2 ounces unsweetened chocolate
> 2 tablespoons (¼ stick) unsalted butter
> 3 cups milk
> ¾ cup sugar
> ½ cup flour
> ¼ teaspoon salt
> 3 egg yolks, slightly beaten
> 1 teaspoon vanilla
>
> ½ pint heavy cream, whipped

Melt chocolate and butter together in small saucepan. Add milk. Combine sugar, flour, and salt in another saucepan. Add chocolate mixture to sugar mixture, stirring over low heat until thick. Add egg yolks and continue cooking for 3 minutes. Remove from heat and stir in vanilla. Let cool slightly and pour into baked 9-inch pie crust or individual crusts. Top with whipped cream at the table.

Note: There will be some custard left over, which keeps for a few days. I like it served ice cold on top of a slice of slightly stale pound cake, which has been sprinkled with rum or brandy first, and topped with whipped cream.

Makes one 9-inch pie

Bulgar salad garnished with romaine lettuce leaves.

Fried chicken wings with a hot and spicy butter sauce.

On the Boat Dock

Dining in a tranquil spot like this on the water invites long, lingering meals—and good conversation. Lots of fresh fruit, nuts, and homemade cookies, plus wine and hot coffee, are a wonderfully relaxing way to end this meal, and the day.

Cold boiled beets with lemon wedges.

On the Boat Dock

MENU
(for 6)

Chicken Wings in Hot Pepper–Butter Sauce
Bulgur Salad
Cold Beets
Toasted Ice-Water Crackers
Assorted Fresh Fruit and Nuts
Pecan Cookies
Wine
Coffee

The salad, beets, and cookies can all be prepared in advance. The crackers can also be made early in the day. This leaves only the chicken wings, which should be served warm. Simplicity itself.

Chicken Wings in Hot Pepper–Butter Sauce

I understand the idea for this combination originated in New York State, but it could have come straight out of Louisiana. The quantity of wings may seem great, but I bet you won't have any left.

3	pounds chicken wings (about 32 pieces)
6	tablespoons (¾ stick) unsalted butter
3	to 10 tablespoons Frank's Louisiana Redhot Sauce
	Oil for frying

Cut off wing tips and discard or reserve for thickening soups. Melt butter and add hot sauce to taste.

Meanwhile, put large skillet on and fill it to a depth of 1 inch with oil (safflower or corn); heat to 375 degrees and drop wings in. Do not crowd. Fry in several batches. Keep them moving and turning until golden, about 10 to 15 minutes. Drain on paper towels.

Brush wings with the butter mixture on both sides. Serve warm. Any leftover sauce can be served on the side.

Serves 6

Bulgur Salad

Bulgur is also called cracked wheat. It is a very popular grain in North Africa and throughout the Middle East. It can be used as a substitute for rice. Here it is soaked in water to make it expand, instead of being cooked.

1¾	cups bulgur wheat
7	cups boiling water
1	medium cucumber, seeded and peeled, cut into small chunks
½	cup minced green onions
2	tablespoons chopped fresh mint leaves
2	large tomatoes, seeded and peeled, coarsely chopped
1	head romaine lettuce

Vinaigrette Dressing

2	teaspoons salt, or to taste
3	tablespoons safflower oil
7	tablespoons olive oil
5	tablespoons lemon juice (fresh only)
	Scant ¼ teaspoon freshly ground black pepper

Put bulgur in a large bowl and pour boiling water over it. Cover and let stand for 2 to 3 hours. Drain off excess water and put into a sieve and shake dry. Return to a serving bowl and add the cucumber, green onion, and mint.

Make a dressing by whisking together the salt, oils, lemon juice, and pepper. Pour this into the salad and mix. Chill, covered, until ready to serve. Before serving, mix in the tomatoes, draining off any liquid that may have accumulated in the container in which they were stored. Garnish with individual leaves of romaine.

Serves 6

Cold Beets

I like to serve these beets along with the Bulgur Salad. They contain no seasoning and just have a squeeze of lemon over them. There is plenty of dressing in with the bulgur. The size of beets and the bunches in which they are tied vary so much that the best way to judge quantity is to allow 4 beets per person if they are small and 2 if they are medium.

  Several bunches beets
2 lemons, cut into wedges

Cut tops from the beets, wash, and cover with water in a saucepan. Bring to a boil. Simmer until tender, 15 to 30 minutes, depending on the size. Let cool in their juice and slip off the skin and root. Serve with lemon wedges.

Toasted Ice-Water Crackers

These crackers have a marvelous flavor and keep especially well in a container with a tight-fitting lid. The flavor even seems to improve in a day or so. They make an ideal accompaniment to soups and lunches and shouldn't require much additional butter.

2 dozen saltine crackers
   Ice water
1/4 cup (1/2 stick) melted butter (or more)

Preheat oven to 400 degrees. Grease a cookie sheet or two.

Have ready a bowl of ice water and the melted butter as well as a small soft brush. Drop the crackers in the water about six at a time. After 28 or 30 seconds, carefully but quickly lift them out, allow water to drip off, and place on a cookie sheet. Do not try to do too many at one time, because by the time you get to the last ones they will have become too soggy. I've found six to be the ideal number. When you have a full cookie sheet, brush each one generously with the melted butter. Don't use too much pressure, because you don't want to flatten the crackers.

Toast in the oven for 10 minutes, then turn heat down to 300 degrees. Continue to toast for an additional 10 to 15 minutes. Cool and store in a container with a tight lid.

Makes 2 dozen crackers

Pecan Cookies

Almost any nuts or combination of nuts can be substituted for the pecans in this recipe.

1/2 cup (1 stick) unsalted butter
3/4 cup light brown sugar, tightly packed
1 egg, beaten
1 1/4 cups all-purpose flour
1/2 teaspoon baking soda
1/2 teaspoon salt
1 teaspoon vanilla
1/2 cup pecans, coarsely chopped

Preheat oven to 375 degrees. Grease 2 cookie sheets.

Cream butter and sugar together. Add the egg and mix well. Sift together the flour, soda, and salt. Add to butter mixture. Add vanilla and 1 teaspoon hot water. Mix. Add pecans and mix.

Drop by rounded teaspoons onto cookie sheets. Bake for 12 minutes, or until golden brown. Remove to a rack and cool.

Makes 3 dozen cookies

Brisket of beef surrounded by a rich onion sauce.

A luscious pear cobbler served with whipped cream.

Soft dinner rolls.

Under the Arbor

A quiet arbor set in a garden filled with flowers is an idyllic place to have an evening meal.

Left: the table set with the brisket, new potatoes, and a salad of beet, endive, and onion.

MENU
(for 6)

Braised and Potted Brisket of Beef
Skillet New Potatoes
Chopped Beet, Endive, and Red Onion Salad
Icebox Rolls and Butter
Pear Cobbler with Whipped Cream
Wine
Coffee

Under the Arbor

I think brisket is my favorite cut of beef. Here it is roasted for a long period and comes out very dark and juicy. The only thing you have to pay attention to is your timing, and even that is flexible. But everything should be ready to go when the rolls come out of the oven so that they can be served hot. The meat can rest for 30 minutes or so after cooking if you have misjudged. Don't forget that the rolls will need up to 1½ hours to rise (maybe less). Plan accordingly. The cobbler is made in the afternoon.

Braised and Potted Brisket of Beef

There are many methods of preparing brisket, some requiring that it spend its whole cooking time covered, but I prefer the dark roasted flavor (instead of steamed) that cooking in this way gives.

	Salt and pepper
4	pounds first-cut fresh brisket
3/4	teaspoon thyme
4	large onions (2 chopped medium and 2 cut into large rings)
1	cup red wine

Preheat oven to 400 degrees.

Salt and pepper meat generously. Put into pan in which meat fits closely. Sprinkle with a bit of the thyme and pack the top with the chopped onions. Put in oven. Turn after 1 hour. Add balance of the thyme and more salt and pepper and continue to cook for 1 hour and 15 minutes.

Put the onion rings on top and sides and add red wine. Cover tightly and cook for another 45 minutes. Test for doneness. It should be fork tender. Total cooking time is 3 hours.

Serves 6

Skillet New Potatoes

Here is the best way I know of cooking new potatoes. It is quick and easy and in one process gives you bits of crispy peel and a soft creamy interior. Also, because they are cooked in a bit of butter, this saves the bother of adding it at the table.

2	pounds small new (red) potatoes
1/2	cup (1 stick) unsalted butter
3	tablespoons water
2	teaspoons salt
1/2	teaspoon pepper

Scrub potatoes and peel a strip around the center of each. (This allows some butter to seep into the potatoes.) Melt butter in deep skillet. Add potatoes, water, salt and pepper. They should be in one layer. Cover and cook over medium to low heat for 25 minutes, shaking the pan occasionally or turning by hand to keep from sticking. If liquid remains in pan at the end of cooking time, reduce so that the potatoes are coated with butter.

Serves 6

Chopped Beet, Endive, and Red Onion Salad

This can be made with canned beets, but they don't compare with the earthy flavor of fresh ones.

	Several bunches of beets
6	medium whole endives
1	medium red onion, peeled and cut into thin rings
	Strong Vinaigrette Dressing (page 153)

Cut off top of beets, leaving roots in place. Cover with water and simmer approximately 30 minutes, or until tender. Allow to cool in juice and slip off skins. Chop into medium-size chunks. Wash and dry endive. Cut into ½-inch rings and separate. Toss beets, endives, and onion together. Dress sparingly with the Strong Vinaigrette.

Serves 6

Icebox Rolls

Soft dinner rolls were very popular when I was growing up. They seem to have fallen out of favor, but I think they are very good along with the rich juices of a brisket of beef. They are easy to prepare, and the leftover dough can be refrigerated and used for up to 3 to 4 days.

1	package dry yeast
1	cup warm water
1/2	cup shortening
1/4	cup sugar
1	egg
1	teaspoon salt
3	cups flour

Preheat oven to 350 degrees.

Dissolve yeast in warm water. Cream shortening with sugar and beat in egg. Add yeast mixture and beat. This will not combine completely but mix well. Add salt and flour, working in until a smooth dough is formed. Knead for a very few minutes. Grease the surface of the dough with a little melted shortening, cover very tightly with plastic wrap, and put in refrigerator.

When ready to use dough, pull off golf-ball-size pieces and roll to make a ball. Refrigerate rest of dough (you will have about half left over) to use another time. Put on greased cookie sheet, cover lightly, and let rise for up to 1 1/2 hours in a warm place. Bake for 15 minutes.

Makes 12 rolls

Pear Cobbler with Whipped Cream

This is a very nice, very simple way to use ripe fresh pears.

6	very large ripe pears
1 1/2	tablespoons lemon juice
	Grated rind of 1/2 lemon
1/4	cup sugar (slightly more if you like)
	Scant 1/4 teaspoon ginger
3/4	teaspoon mace
	Generous 1/4 teaspoon chopped fresh mint

Batter

1	cup all-purpose flour
1/2	cup sugar
1	teaspoon baking powder
1/4	teaspoon salt
2	egg yolks
1/4	cup milk
1	tablespoon melted unsalted butter
1/2	pint heavy cream, whipped with 1 teaspoon vanilla

Preheat oven to 375 degrees. Grease 1 1/2- to 2-quart ovenproof dish and set aside.

Peel and core the pears. Cut into medium chunks. Pour lemon juice over pears and add grated rind. Mix. Combine sugar, spices, and mint, add to pears, and mix. Put in baking dish.

Mix batter by combining flour, sugar, baking powder, and salt and sifting into a bowl. Beat egg yolks and milk together and mix with flour. Add melted butter and then pour batter over fruit. Bake for 30 minutes. Serve with flavored whipped cream.

Note: This dish can look quite done on the top and still be raw in the middle. Be sure to test for doneness by lifting a piece of the fruit from the center. Turn down heat and bake longer if necessary.

Serves 6

In the
Dining
Room

In the Dining Room

MENU
(for 8)

Chicken Sausage Patties
Skillet-Baked Corn
Turnip Greens with Hot Pepper Vinegar
and Cornmeal Dumplings
Pear and Turnip Purée
Bread Pudding with Peach Sauce
Wine
Coffee

This menu includes a few pleasant surprises that have their roots solidly planted in the South. The sausages must be made a day in advance and the dumplings done last; otherwise, it is a pretty flexible meal as far as timing is concerned. The pudding can be made in the afternoon. The turnip greens reheat very well and can be cooked several hours before. The purée cooks while the corn is baking. The dumplings go in when the corn does. The chicken patties only take 8 to 10 minutes to finish, and they will hold for another 10 or 15.

Preceding page: *This charming little dining room, with the late afternoon light coming through its open window, is enough to lure anyone inside to dine—no matter how fabulous the view outside.*

Chicken Sausage Patties

The spice and herb combinations in sausage are a wonderful complement to strong vegetables such as turnip greens, which are a part of this menu.

This recipe for making sausage with chicken is very simple. It should be made a day in advance and refrigerated uncooked to give the flavors a chance to develop. After you have made the sausages once, you might want to try varying the seasonings to find a taste that is uniquely your own. When experimenting, though, make quarter batches, because sausage seasoning is tricky. Many recipes suggest you pinch off a small quantity of the finished mix and fry it to tell if it needs altering.

	Generous 1 cup uncooked, noninstant rice (2 cups cooked)
	Grated rind of 1/2 large lemon
3/4	teaspoon each of ground sage, thyme, and poultry seasoning
3/4	teaspoon freshly ground black pepper
	Dash of cayenne pepper
1	teaspoon salt
1/2	cup clarified unsalted butter
2	pounds boned chicken breast, coarsely ground

Cook rice according to directions. You should have 2 cups. Drain well and run hot water over to rinse off excess starch. Put in a crockery bowl and add lemon rind, herbs, peppers, and salt. Pour over it the clarified butter, which has been allowed to cool. Toss lightly. Add chicken and mix with your hands. Divide into 2 equal portions and shape into rolls. Wrap tightly in foil. Refrigerate at least 24 hours before using.

To cook, cut each roll into 8 patties and put in a warm skillet that has been rubbed with a few drops of safflower oil. Turn up heat and brown on each side. The patties cook very fast, the whole cooking time being about 8 minutes. Put on a platter and pour over any butter that may have rendered out. Keep warm.

Makes 16 patties

Skillet-Baked Corn

This method of cooking corn gives it a wonderfully nutty and chewy crust. There are several ways of frying corn, but I think this is the least bother and gives the best results. When this dish is stir-fried on top of the stove with a few green peppers and chopped green onions it is called "Indian corn" or "Mexican corn." The name doesn't matter. If you like corn, you will love this.

The most important things about the preparation are the use of proper skillets and the preheating of them. I use two very well-seasoned 8-inch iron skillets. The oven is turned up to 425 degrees, and the oiled skillets are put inside to heat for a 1/2 hour while the oven preheats.

4	tablespoons safflower oil
16	good-size ears of white corn
1	teaspoon salt
1	cup flour

Put 2 tablespoons safflower oil in each of 2 heavy 8-inch iron skillets and put into the oven set for 425 degrees. Allow to heat for 30 minutes.

Cut kernels from the corn cobs and scrape thoroughly to get out all the juice. Add salt and stir. Add flour, stirring constantly. This will make a thick batter.

Take a heated skillet out of the oven and put half the corn mixture in the middle of the pan. Do not stir, but spread out into pan and place back in the oven. Repeat with the other pan. Cook for 30 minutes, or until a nice crust forms on the bottom and the top is beginning to brown. Remove from the oven and invert over serving plate. Cut into wedges. This can be rather crumbly, so serve carefully, using a spatula and a fork.

Serves 8

Turnip Greens with Hot Pepper Vinegar and Cornmeal Dumplings

You don't often find turnip greens at farm stands, but where there are locally grown turnips, there are greens. Just ask the owner of the stand to gather them for you. If none is available, you might substitute collard, mustard greens, or kale. In a pinch you can always use frozen greens, but frozen vegetables in the midst of the abundant produce of summer and fall seems an affront.

Some people, and this includes me, like to sprinkle a little Hot Pepper Vinegar on their serving of greens.

3	pounds turnip greens
2	medium onions, coarsely chopped
1	1/4-pound strip salt pork
1	teaspoon salt
	Freshly ground pepper to taste

Dumplings

1	cup yellow cornmeal
1/4	cup flour
1	teaspoon baking powder
1/2	teaspoon salt
2	eggs
1/2	cup milk
1	tablespoon melted unsalted butter

Put turnip greens in cold water and strip out all stems and brown spots. Drain and tear into small pieces. Put greens, onions, pork, salt, and pepper in a pan and pour water in just to cover. The greens will cook down considerably, so you should force them down into the pot before covering with water. Cover and simmer for 45 minutes. Let stand in juice.

Combine all dry ingredients for dumplings and mix well. Drain greens, catching liquid in a bowl. Return liquid to pan and bring to a simmer. Keep greens warm. Beat eggs and milk lightly and add slowly to dry ingredients, stirring as you do. Stir in melted butter.

Drop batter from spoon into greens liquid and cover pan tightly. Simmer for 15 minutes. Remove dumplings and keep warm. Put greens back in liquid to heat, then pour, liquid and all, into serving bowl. Serve immediately with Hot Pepper Vinegar.

Serves 8

Hot Pepper Vinegar

	Small bottle red wine vinegar
3	or 4 hot peppers

Buy a small bottle of red wine vinegar with a sprinkler top. Pour out a bit of the vinegar and force 3 or 4 cut hot peppers into the bottle, including the seeds. Pour vinegar back into the bottle to fill. Allow to marinate for several days before using. This concoction gets more potent with time. After using this once, you may wish to increase the number of peppers. It is also good on scrambled eggs.

Chicken sausage with dumplings and skillet corn. Turnip greens and pear-turnip purée in background.

A light and cool bread pudding is served with a sauce made from fresh, ripe peaches.

Old wicker furniture and geraniums on this lovely open porch seem to spell summer.

Pear and Turnip Purée

The flavor of turnips can be especially strong, so I like to add something to the purée to reduce their bitterness. This combination was suggested to me by Christopher Idone a few years back. I think it is an unusually successful marriage of flavors. Several small boiled white potatoes are also good mashed into the turnips in place of the pears. In that case, omit the sugar.

2½ pounds turnips
4   firm pears
½   lemon, cut into 2 parts
4   to 6 tablespoons unsalted butter (to taste)
1   tablespoon sugar
    Salt and pepper

Peel and cut the turnips into 1-inch cubes and steam until fork tender.

While the turnips are cooking, peel and core the pears. Cut in half and put in a saucepan, just covered with water. Add cut lemon pieces. Bring to a simmer. Cook just a few minutes, until tender; do not overcook. Let stand in the water.

When the turnips are done, purée them with the butter and sugar. Remove pears carefully to a strainer and drain for a few minutes, pressing slightly against the strainer to remove more of the liquid. Discard water and lemon. Add pears to puréed turnips and purée briefly. Add salt and pepper to taste. If not serving immediately, reheat later in top of double boiler.

Serves 8

Bread Pudding with Peach Sauce

This bread pudding is very light because it calls for low-fat milk instead of cream and whole milk. Its cool flavor is especially pleasant after the foregoing spicy meal.

½   cup (1 stick) unsalted butter, softened
10 or more 1-inch slices day-old French bread with crusts removed
4   eggs
¾   cup plus 2 tablespoons sugar
4   cups low-fat milk
2   teaspoons vanilla extract
    Freshly grated nutmeg

Sauce
6   ripe peaches
4   tablespoons sugar
    Juice of ½ large lemon

Preheat oven to 350 degrees.

Grease a small ovenproof casserole with butter. Spread the remainder of the butter on one side of the bread slices. Put them in the casserole. If this is not enough bread to cover the bottom of the casserole, add a few more slices.

Beat eggs and ¾ cup sugar in a large bowl. Pour in the milk, stirring. Add vanilla extract and stir. Add a few good grinds of nutmeg.

Pour the mixture carefully through a strainer into the casserole. The bread will float to the top. Sprinkle a tablespoon or more of sugar over the bread. Put casserole in a larger ovenproof pan and surround with enough boiling water to come ½ inch up the sides of the casserole. Put pan in the center of the oven and reduce the heat to 325 degrees. Bake for 45 minutes.

To make topping, dip peaches into boiling water for four or five seconds to loosen the skins. Peel and pit and cut into 5 or 6 slices each. Put in a bowl and sprinkle with sugar and lemon juice. Stir and refrigerate, covered. Before serving, purée. If not sweet enough, add more sugar. More lemon juice may be added, too, although it is used here just to help keep the peaches from discoloring while they are being refrigerated.

Serves 8

Peach Crisp with Bourbon Sauce*

Since the preparation and timing of the dumplings, corn, and sausage patties in this menu might be the focus of your attention here, I am including this alternate dessert. It is somewhat easier to prepare than the Bread Pudding, but if you do substitute it, be sure to try the pudding at a later date. It is delicious. The peach dish should be made only when the fruit is at the height of its season as it depends almost entirely on the peaches for its flavor and sweetness. It is best if it is not too sweet because it is served with a Bourbon Sauce that is sweet. This sauce could be used on the Bread Pudding if the peaches called for in that recipe are not available or are not of good quality. Should the sauce not appeal to you, you might like sweetened whipped cream or ice cream in its place.

7	large peaches, sliced thin
	Juice of 1 lemon
	Grated rind of 1/2 lemon
1/4	teaspoon nutmeg (optional)
1/3	cup unsalted butter
1	cup sifted flour
3/4	cup rolled oats
1	cup brown sugar, tightly packed
1/2	cup pecans or walnuts, coarsely chopped (optional)

Preheat oven to 325 degrees. Butter a 9 × 9-inch ovenproof dish.

Dip peaches in boiling water for 30 seconds. Skin and pit them. Slice thin and place in the prepared baking dish. Sprinkle with lemon juice and grated rind. (You may also add 1/4 teaspoon nutmeg if you like.)

Cut butter into 8 to 10 pieces and combine with all the other ingredients except the nuts. Mix together using a pastry blender or two knives. When it is crumbly, work in the nuts if you are using them. Pour the topping over the peaches and press down to cover evenly. Bake for 30 minutes or until peaches are tender. Serve at room temperature with the following sauce.

Serves 8

Alternate to Bread Pudding recipe

Bourbon Sauce*

In the part of the South where I grew up there was a distinct preference for dessert sauces containing spirits. Even some of our popular drinks, such as eggnog and the revered mint julep, come very close to being confections.

1/2	cup (1 stick) unsalted butter
1	cup superfine sugar
1	egg
1/2	cup bourbon, more or less, depending on taste

Cut butter into small pieces and place in a double boiler over hot but not boiling water. While this is melting, beat the egg lightly and combine it with the superfine sugar. Pour this mixture into the melted butter and cook for several minutes until the sugar granules disappear and egg is cooked, being careful not to let the water boil. The reason for not allowing the water to boil is to keep the egg from curdling; however, you should not have that much trouble. Remove from the hot water and add bourbon after it has cooled. Serve at room temperature.

Makes 2 cups

Alternate to Peach Sauce recipe

On the Terrace

A delectable harvest dinner fills a round table on this lovely brick terrace: boiled smoked pork butt on a platter surrounded by plentiful fall vegetables, mustards, horseradish, and dark breads and butter.

For dessert, a fresh-tasting green tomato and apple pie served with cream.

On the Terrace

This menu is a fall treat, when vegetables are so plentiful. The only problem it presents for me is one of restraint. I always want to throw every vegetable in sight into the pot. However, no matter how many are added, this is still essentially a single-dish dinner. The only caution I might offer is not to overcook the vegetables.

Boiled Smoked Pork Butt with Vegetables

This dish can be done in two parts. The meat can be boiled first and reheated just before serving time and the vegetables put in for their 15 minutes at the end.

2	small smoked pork butts
2	bay leaves
3	medium white potatoes, cut into 1-inch cubes
3	medium sweet potatoes, cut into 1-inch cubes
2	kohlrabies, cut into ½-inch rings
2	parsnips, cut into ½-inch rings
12	small skinned white onions
2	turnips, cut into 1-inch cubes
1	small head cabbage, cut into 8 wedges
8	small tender pieces of celery, trimmed and left whole
½	cup (1 stick) unsalted butter

Cover pork butt with water, add bay leaves, and simmer for 1½ to 2 hours, or until fork tender. Remove the meat to a platter and keep warm.

Return liquid to a boil. Put vegetables in the boiling liquid, finish with the cabbage and celery on top. (The best way to peel white onions is to simmer them in boiling water for a couple of minutes. Remove and cut off root and the skins will slide off.) Be careful not to separate the cabbage. Steam and simmer for 15 to 20 minutes, until done, being careful not to overcook.

While vegetables are steaming, melt butter. Arrange sliced meat and vegetables on a platter, pour butter over the vegetables, and serve.

Serves 6–8

Mustard and Horseradish

Use a good strong mustard and freshly grated or bottled horseradish, mixed with a little heavy cream if you like. Put mustard and horseradish in separate serving bowls.

Apple and Green Tomato Pie with Cream

The green tomatoes used here give this American classic a new twist. This recipe makes a thin and runny pie, which is the way I like it. Fruit pies that call for an agent to thicken the juice become too heavy to suit me and tend to lose that fresh fruit taste I like. This pie will have to be served from the pan in which it is baked. The first piece will be a mess, but plunge ahead. It gets neater.

Pie Crust
1½   cups flour
      Scant ¼ teaspoon salt
9   tablespoons (1 stick plus 1 tablespoon) frozen unsalted butter
4   to 5 tablespoons ice water

Filling
1   cup sugar
¼   teaspoon salt
½   teaspoon cinnamon
1   tablespoon grated lemon rind
2   cups peeled, cored, and thinly sliced McIntosh or greening apples
2   cups thinly sliced green tomatoes, with any large seeds removed
1   tablespoon fresh lemon juice
½   cup (1 stick) unsalted butter, cut into thin strips

      Fresh cream, whipped cream, or ice cream

To make pastry, put flour and salt in a food processor. Add butter and process until butter is the size of small peas. Add 4 to 5 tablespoons ice water and process until dough begins to cling together, no longer. Gather into a ball and divide into 2 parts. Make a flattened ball with one part and wrap it in waxed paper and refrigerate. Line a small 8-inch pie pan with the other piece, which has been rolled thin on a floured surface. Trim and refrigerate, covered, until ready to use.

Preheat oven to 450 degrees.

To make filling, put sugar, salt, cinnamon, and lemon rind in a bowl. Mix. Add apples and tomatoes and toss. Add lemon juice and toss lightly. Pile mixture into the prepared pastry, mounding the middle. Put slices of butter on top.

Remove second ball of crust from refrigerator and roll out thin. Cover the apple mixture. Seal with tines of a fork and cut holes for steam. Brush with cream to make crust brown more, if you like. (You may also sprinkle the top with more sugar.) Put in preheated oven and bake for 10 minutes. Turn oven down to 350 degrees and continue to bake for another 35 minutes. Remove to a rack to cool. Serve with fresh cream, whipped cream, or ice cream.

Makes one 8-inch pie

By Firelight

In winter, if you are lucky enough to have a fireplace, set up everything on the coffee table.

MENU
(for 6)

Fresh Ham with Pan Gravy
Sautéed Okra, Tomatoes, and Corn
Fettuccini Soufflé
Endive Salad
Peach Cobbler with Whipped Cream
Wine   Coffee

Peach cobbler with fresh whipped cream.

Although fresh ham is simple to cook, its baking time is long. This means planning ahead carefully. Luckily, its texture improves by allowing it to rest for 30 minutes after being taken from the oven. This grace period gives you the option of finishing the meal leisurely and with flexibility. When the ham comes out of the oven, the Fettuccini Soufflé goes in. The okra dish is very good just warm, so that presents no problem, and the endive can be chopped and dressed while the fettuccini bakes. The dessert will have been made late in the afternoon.

By Firelight

Fresh Ham with Pan Gravy

Any leftover ham and gravy you might have after serving this meal can become the main ingredient for a potpie. Try it with a cornmeal crust. However, if this is not your plan, don't buy a whole ham. Remember Dorothy Parker's definition of eternity: "Two people and a ham."

1	8- to 9-pound ham (fresh only)
	Salt and pepper
1½	cups chicken stock
½	cup (1 stick) unsalted butter, melted
¾	teaspoon dry mustard
1	tablespoon lemon juice
¼	teaspoon thyme

Preheat oven to 325 degrees.

Place ham on a rack and salt and pepper generously. You may also dust lightly with flour. Put in the oven. Cook 25 minutes to the pound and baste every 30 minutes or so with ½ cup of the chicken stock and a mixture of the butter, mustard, lemon juice, and thyme.

Pour off all the grease from the pan and pour in the remaining 1 cup chicken stock and deglaze the pan. You may also add any leftover basting liquid. Simmer a few minutes. If desired, thicken the gravy by using 2 tablespoons flour made into a paste with 1 tablespoon soft butter. Simmer for 15 minutes if you do this, and correct seasoning.

Serves 6

Sautéed Okra, Tomatoes, and Corn

Okra for some is an acquired taste. If you are one of those, you might start by trying this recipe. I've found most people's objection has vaguely to do with its viscous texture, and most of that is cooked away here. What is left combines wonderfully with onions and tomatoes.

This dish can be served hot or just warm. Personally, I prefer the latter, because the flavors seem at their most distinct. Another advantage serving it like this is that you can make it ahead of your other preparations and get it out of the way.

If you have limited time or you have had enough corn for the season, you can do without it.

2	pounds okra, stem and tips removed
3	pounds tomatoes, skinned and seeded
1	pound onions, coarsely chopped
8	ears fresh corn
2	tablespoons clarified unsalted butter
2	tablespoons safflower oil
3	teaspoons salt
	Freshly ground black pepper to taste

Cut okra into ¼-inch rounds, discarding the stems and tops. Set aside. There should be approximately 6 cups.

Dip tomatoes into boiling water for 5 seconds. Skin, remove stem end, and squeeze out the seeds and some juice. Put in a stainless or enameled pan and cook slowly for approximately ½ hour to get rid of some excess water. Do not scorch. There should be approximately 2 cups of reduced pulp when finished. Pour off any excess water before measuring.

Peel onions and chop coarsely. There should be approximately 4 cups.

Cut corn off the cob with a sharp knife. Hold shucked ear broad end down on a cutting board and cut kernels off with a downward movement. It is not necessary to cut too deeply, as you can scrape off with the dull side of the knife what pulp is left on the ear. There should be approximately 4 cups of kernels and pulp.

Heat butter and safflower oil in a large deep skillet. When medium hot, add the okra and onions together. Cook until onions are completely wilted and okra has begun to brown on the edges. Turn and scrape the bottom of the pan often with a spatula. This can take from 10 to 15 minutes. Add reduced tomatoes and salt. Simmer for 5 minutes. There should not be too much liquid from the tomatoes in the pan. Pour out excess if tomatoes have not been drained properly.

Add corn and scraped pulp, cooking just long enough to heat the corn thoroughly, approximately 3 or 4 minutes. Add pepper, and more salt if desired.

Note: You will have enough leftovers for a delicious vegetable lunch. A little Hot Pepper Vinegar (see page 129) sprinkled over the top is very good.

Serves 6, with leftovers

Fettuccini Soufflé

This is a fairly stable soufflé that will hold its shape longer than the more tender ones, but it is still best to time your meal so that you can get everyone to the table when it is due to come out.

½	pound fresh fettuccini
1⅓	cups milk
1	clove garlic, peeled and finely minced
½	cup plus 3 tablespoons grated Parmesan cheese
¼	pound Fontina cheese, grated (½ cup grated)
½	cup (1 stick) unsalted butter, cut into small pieces
	Salt and pepper
1	to 2 teaspoons chopped parsley
6	large eggs, separated

Preheat the oven to 350 degrees. Grease a 1½- to 2-quart soufflé dish.

Cook fettuccini al dente, about 3 or 4 minutes, in rapidly boiling salted water. Cook less if pasta is very fresh. Drain.

Bring milk to a boil while pasta is cooking. Mix drained fettuccini with hot milk, garlic, ½ cup Parmesan cheese, Fontina, and butter. Season with salt and pepper to taste. Add parsley. Let cool about 30 minutes.

Add egg yolks to cooled fettuccini mixture and blend. Beat egg whites with a pinch of salt until stiff. Fold carefully into fettuccini mixture. Dust the inside of the buttered soufflé dish with 3 tablespoons Parmesan cheese and pour the mixture in. Bake for approximately 45 minutes. During last 5 minutes, turn the oven up to 425 degrees to form a crusty top.

Serves 6

Endive Salad

Allow 2 small endives per guest, or 1 large each. Wash them carefully and cut into small rings so that they will be easier to eat. If this is done too early they will tend to turn slightly dark, so it is a good idea to toss them with a good squeeze of lemon to protect their color.

Make the following dressing: Whisk together 2 tablespoons fresh lemon juice, 1 teaspoon salt, a dash of freshly ground black pepper, 2 tablespoons safflower oil, and 4 tablespoons *good* light olive oil.

Makes ½ cup dressing

Peach Cobbler with Whipped Cream

Make this cobbler when peaches are at the peak of their season. It is about as simple as a dessert can be.

Cobbler batter

1½	cup all purpose flour
	scant ¼ teaspoon salt
5	tablespoons frozen, unsalted butter
4	tablespoons frozen Crisco
4	to 5 tablespoons ice water
7	very large ripe peaches, skinned and pitted
1	cup sugar
¼	cup (½ stick) unsalted butter
½	pint heavy cream, whipped, or light cream

Preheat oven to 450 degrees. Lightly grease a 1½- to 2-quart dish.

To make cobbler batter, place flour and salt in a food processor. Add butter and Crisco and process until shortening is the size of small peas. Add 4 tablespoons ice water and process until dough begins to cling together (this shouldn't take too long—10 seconds or so). If more water is required, add it. Gather dough into a ball. Wrap in plastic wrap or wax paper. Refrigerate until ready to use.

Roll out the pastry into a large ragged circle. Since handling this large circle of dough can be difficult, dust it with flour and roll up on your rolling pin (window shade fashion). Unroll over the prepared dish. Carefully slip it down into the dish so that you have lined the bottom and sides, allowing the excess to hang over if necessary.

Cut the peaches into 8 or 9 slices and heap into the dish. Cover with sugar and dot with butter. Flop the loose ends of the pastry over the top. Any extra loose pieces of dough you have can be used to fill in. Put in preheated oven and turn down to 425 degrees. Bake for 45 minutes. Let cool and serve with whipped or plain cream.

Serves 6

A leisurely Sunday lunch on the deck at my house is followed in the evening by a barbecue. The same setting looks very different as the light changes and the table is moved down to the water's edge.

THE LONG

WEEKEND

The Long Weekend

While I genuinely like to cook, I must admit that after three days of it I have pretty much had enough, so I plan for a longer weekend—like the Fourth of July or Labor Day—a bit differently. Usually I count it a success if I don't have any leftovers to deal with after a meal; however, this is one time I *like* having them. I know that freezing food is very popular, but personally, I don't freeze many things. I find that freezing absolutely destroys the flavor of most cooked meats and the texture of all vegetables and fruits. So the only thing I have to fall back on is "fresh" leftovers.

I also try for more variety on longer weekends. For instance, in the plan that follows, the first menu, for Friday dinner, is built around brisket of beef, followed on Saturday by an all-vegetable lunch and then a vaguely Japanese fish dinner. The brisket reappears for lunch on Sunday with a surprise or two thrown in, followed that evening by a barbecue. For the final Monday lunch we all go on a diet. A word of caution though: Variety is important, but don't overdo. Remember you have more days to go than usual, so pace yourself. When you get to Sunday lunch, for example, if you are tired or harried or both, skip the poached bananas and buy some sherbet for dessert. Omit the eggs in crumb cups and just hard-boil some eggs, slice them, and dab their tops with some sort of bought chunky tomato hot sauce. I'll say again, if you are not having fun, chances are your guests will feel it, so the extra effort expended can actually be counterproductive.

Mapping out menus for a whole weekend at one time will help you decide on what quantities to buy. It is important to understand that when using leftovers (note that I refer here only to lunch; I never make leftovers part of the evening meal) a very little goes a long way when you offer enough choices. Everyone has a taste of many things, which together add up to a whole meal. And when you have my standbys on hand (cheese, bread, tomatoes), almost anything will be worth sending around a second time.

Friday Dinner

Left: *Friday dinner is set out on a scrubbed pine table. The view is from my kitchen into the glass-enclosed dining room.*

Blackberry cobbler.

The brisket in this menu has to cook for 3 or 4 hours, so be sure to put it on early enough. It can sit in its broth for up to an hour after it is done if things are not working out on schedule. If you can, make the cobbler in the afternoon so that it will be out of the way. It's delicious when just warm, but better to save such treats for when they would be most appreciated and you have more leisure—like a rainy afternoon. The horseradish sauce can be made

early, too, as it reheats well. Peel and prepare all the raw vegetables before anyone arrives, and set aside in water. Do the same for all the dry corn bread ingredients.

About an hour before you want to serve, start finishing the vegetables and put the corn bread pans in to heat with the oven. Everything will hold pretty well for 10 or 15 minutes while you are getting it all organized. Call for help if you find yourself doing two things at once.

Friday Dinner

Boiled Brisket of Beef

Brisket is generally available most places, but if you are planning a weekend around it, it's a good idea to call ahead of time and arrange to have your butcher get one especially for you. You can either use the first cut, which is thinner and leaner, or the second, which is thick and contains more fat. Naturally, the first cut costs a bit more. This recipe calls for 6 pounds of meat, but if you are planning on leftovers you might want to use more.

6   pounds brisket of beef
2   medium onions, peeled and stuck with 2 cloves
2   unpeeled onions, washed and broken into several pieces
1   tablespoon kosher salt
2   bay leaves
4   sprigs parsley
     Few sprigs fresh thyme or 1 teaspoon dried
4   celery stalks, with leaves broken in several pieces

Put meat in a large kettle, cover with water, and add all other ingredients. Bring to a boil, reduce heat, and simmer, covered, for 3 to 4 hours. It should be just tender but not falling apart. Skim a few times during the cooking and keep an eye on it to keep it from boiling over. I keep the lid slightly ajar. During the cooking time the meat will shrink and float up, so you might want to turn it a time or two.

Leave it in the essence until ready to carve. It can stay this way for up to an hour. Store and reheat any leftovers in this juice, too.

Serves 6, with leftovers

Horseradish Sauce

This sauce adds just enough zip to the beef to make it really delicious. Be sure that the onions are browned lightly, as they add a distinctive flavor.

¼   cup (½ stick) unsalted butter, melted
2   cups chicken stock
½   cup finely chopped onion
2   tablespoons flour
1   tablespoon lemon juice
¼   teaspoon white pepper
4   or more tablespoons prepared horseradish

Melt butter in saucepan. Put the chicken stock on to heat. Add the onion to the butter and brown lightly. Add the flour and mix well, then add the hot stock. Stir and simmer for a few minutes to thicken. Mix in the lemon juice and pepper and simmer over very low heat for 10 minutes. Add the horseradish last. Taste for seasoning. This can cool and be reheated later.

Makes approximately 2 cups sauce

Green Bean and Potato Purée

This dish is a winner. It also can hold for a few minutes while you get everything else ready to serve.

1   pound white potatoes, peeled and cut into cubes
2   teaspoons salt
1   pound green beans, tips off, broken into several pieces
5   tablespoons unsalted butter
     Freshly grated nutmeg to taste

Preheat oven to 450 degrees.

Put potato cubes in a saucepan and cover with water; add salt. Bring to a boil and add the green beans. Cook for approximately 10 minutes. The beans should be just getting tender.

Drain and put into a food processor fitted with a metal blade. Purée, scraping down a few times. Add 4 tablespoons butter, cut into bits, and mix. Add nutmeg, and correct seasoning.

Pour into a baking dish and top with the remaining butter, cut into small pieces. Bake for 20 minutes. Serve from the baking dish.

Serves 6

Honey Carrots

Carrots prepared this way can sit for 10 minutes or so after they are done, but should not wait too much longer, as they begin to lose their flavor.

- 4 generous cups carrots, peeled and cut into thin rounds
- 4 generous tablespoons honey
- 2 tablespoons plus 2 teaspoons unsalted butter
- 1/4 teaspoon salt
- 1/2 teaspoon nutmeg
- 3 tablespoons lemon juice

Mix all ingredients in a skillet with a tightly fitting lid. Cook over moderate high heat until the liquid evaporates and the carrots begin to just brown. If they are tender and there is still liquid in the pan, remove the cover and boil it out rapidly. The timing on this can vary greatly, depending on the thickness of the rings and the age of the carrots—ten minutes more or less.

Serves 6

Cornsticks

To make these successfully, there are two very important things to remember. You must have a pair of seasoned black iron stick-pans, and these pans, with oil in each slot, must be smoking hot when you put the batter in.

- 2½ tablespoons cooking oil
- 2 cups white cornmeal
- 4 teaspoons baking powder
- 1½ teaspoons salt
- 1 egg
- 1½ cups milk

Turn on oven to 450 degrees ½ hour before you plan to bake the sticks. Prepare the pans by putting ½ teaspoon oil in each slot. Put the pans in to heat up.

When the pans are hot, put the cornmeal, baking powder, and salt in a bowl and mix. Beat the egg lightly and add it to the milk. Mix the dry and liquid ingredients together very quickly. Do not overmix.

Remove the first pan. Be sure to have a heatproof pad or board ready to set it down on, as the pan can scorch the top of a counter. Fill each slot, using a tablespoon. It will puff up to fill. Do not overfill. Put the filled pan in the oven and repeat with the second pan. Bake for 20 minutes. Take from oven and remove the sticks carefully with a fork. Loosen any batter that has overflowed and hardened around the edges. They should then pop right out. If one doesn't come out immediately, move on quickly to the next one and come back to the reluctant one when you have finished and the pan has cooled slightly.

Makes 16 cornsticks

Blackberry Cobbler

Blackberries grow wild in most areas of the country where there are damp spots or streams. They are delectable when cooked in a cobbler and fun to find and pick growing wild.

- 1 recipe cobbler batter (page 141)
- 6 cups blackberries, washed
- 3/4 cup sugar
- 1/4 cup (½ stick) unsalted butter

    Fresh cream, whipped cream, or ice cream

Preheat oven to 425 degrees. Have ready a 9-inch round ovenproof dish 2 inches or more deep. Prepare dough and refrigerate while you get everything else ready.

Roll out dough into a large ragged circle, big enough to line pan and flop over the top. This will not completely cover top.

After lining pan, dump in the berries and pour the sugar over them. Dot generously with the butter. Bring the edges of the pastry over the berries. There will probably be a little space in the center. If you have any pieces of dough that fell off, you can use them to fill in. They don't have to join the other pieces. Edna Lewis, one of my favorite cookbook authors, suggests crushing a few sugar cubes and sprinkling them on top. This is a very nice touch.

Bake in preheated oven for 45 minutes. It is best to put a sheet of foil in the bottom of the oven, as cobblers tend to bubble over. Allow to cool and serve with fresh cream, whipped cream, or ice cream.

Serves 6

Saturday Lunch

My favorite all-vegetable lunch served on the deck: steamed new potatoes, asparagus, and artichokes with lemon wedges; broccoli, green beans, tomatoes with fresh mayonnaise; olives and green onions; braised sweet red peppers in olive oil; strong vinaigrette dressing; hard-boiled pheasant eggs; jalapeño corn bread; and, for dessert, strawberries in lemon juice and sugar, with champagne grapes to nibble.

Saturday Lunch

Assorted Vegetables

These do not have to be done in any particular order. Just plunge in when you have a free moment.

> New potatoes
> Broccoli
> Asparagus
> Artichokes
> Green beans
> Sweet red peppers
> Tomatoes

Scrub the potatoes, cover with water, and bring to a boil. Cook for about 15 minutes, or until tender. Leave in skins.

Clean broccoli and cut off the tough stem and leaves. Divide into sections, leaving flowerets intact. Stand on their ends in a steamer and steam until just fork tender. This can be as little as several minutes depending on the age and freshness of vegetable. It is better to undercook than overcook in this case.

Trim off hard end of the asparagus and peel away the skin about an inch up from the bottom. A potato peeler can be used for this. Steam for only 3 or 4 minutes, tied in a bunch and standing upright. Do not overcook.

Cut off the artichoke stems even with the bottom and trim the sticky end of each leaf straight across, cutting away about ½ inch. Soak covered with cool water for about 30 minutes. Drain and cover with fresh water and simmer 10 to 15 minutes. Test for doneness by poking the cut-off bottom with a fork to see if it has gotten tender. Drain and set aside.

Snip off stem ends of green beans and plunge into boiling salted water. Cook only until crisp-tender.

Grill the whole red peppers under the broiler until they are completely blackened. Store in a paper bag with the top folded over until ready to peel, seed, and quarter.

Dip the tomatoes in hot water for 4 or 5 seconds. Refrigerate, unpeeled, until ready to slice.

Boil pheasant eggs 10 minutes. Drain and place in a bowl of cold water.

MENU
(for 6)

Assorted Vegetables: New Potatoes, Broccoli, Asparagus, Artichokes, Green Beans, Braised Sweet Red Peppers, Tomatoes, Olives, Green Onions

Hard-Boiled Pheasant Eggs

Homemade Mayonnaise

Strong Vinaigrette Dressing

Jalapeño Corn Bread

Marinated Strawberries   Champagne Grapes

Wine

Iced Tea

Except for the strawberries, which should be chilled, everything here should be served at room temperature, including the corn bread. This means that you can do these vegetables anytime you like. It is, however, best to do them so that they don't have to be refrigerated if you can avoid it. I always include a starchy vegetable along with the others and some sort of bread or cracker, but any combination is good. I also think it is best to steam everything at least lightly. Potatoes, of course, should be cooked through. Mayonnaise and Strong Vinaigrette as well as plain light olive oil and vinegar complete the menu.

This is the sort of all-vegetable lunch I'm partial to. If you would prefer to serve meat with it, serve thin-sliced ham (store-bought).

Homemade Mayonnaise

3 tablespoons plus 1 teaspoon fresh lemon juice
2 generous teaspoons green peppercorn mustard
2 teaspoons salt
1/2 teaspoon white pepper
1 egg
2 drops Tabasco sauce
1 1/2 cups safflower oil
1/2 cup mild olive oil

Put all ingredients except oils into bowl of a food processor fitted with a metal blade. Put top in place and turn on machine. Pour oils into mixture in a steady stream through the feed tube (with the motor still running). Add a few more drops of lemon juice or a bit more salt if necessary. Refrigerate in a covered jar until ready to use. This holds its flavor for 4 or 5 days. It will start to taste a bit metallic after that.

To serve with vegetables you may want to mix a small amount of chopped parsley in with 1/2 cup of the finished mayonnaise.

Makes 2 1/2 cups

Strong Vinaigrette

1 teaspoon salt, or to taste
Generous 1 teaspoon green peppercorn mustard, more to taste
Scant 1/2 teaspoon freshly ground pepper
2 tablespoons balsamic vinegar
3 tablespoons plus 1 teaspoon safflower oil
2 tablespoons mild olive oil

Whisk the first four ingredients together, then add the oils and continue whisking until well blended. Refrigerate until ready to use. If you have time, always let dressing come to room temperature before serving.

Makes 1/2 cup dressing

Jalapeño Corn Bread

Jalapeño peppers are quite hot, so unless you are accustomed to them, don't go overboard. After handling the peppers be sure to wash your hands thoroughly, and do not rub your eyes. The hot juice lingers.

2/3 cup safflower oil
2 eggs, lightly beaten
1 1/2-pound carton sour cream
1 16-ounce can creamed corn
2 tablespoons minced or grated onion
2 tablespoons chopped bell peppers
2 jalapeño peppers, chopped fine
1 1/2 cups yellow cornmeal
2 teaspoons baking powder
1 teaspoon salt
1 cup grated sharp Cheddar cheese

Preheat oven to 350 degrees. Oil a 9-inch skillet or heavy pan.

Mix safflower oil, eggs, sour cream, and creamed corn. Mix in the onion, bell peppers, and jalapeños.

Mix the dry ingredients and pour the liquid ingredients in. Mix quickly, leaving a few lumps.

Pour half the batter into the prepared pan. Top with the cheese. Cover with the remaining batter. Bake 45 minutes. Let cool for at least 10 minutes before unmolding or serving directly from the pan.

Serves 6

Marinated Strawberries

Strawberries are served this way all over Italy. The lemon juice combines wonderfully with the strawberries.

2 pints strawberries, washed, hulled, and sliced in two
3 tablespoons granulated sugar
3 tablespoons fresh lemon juice

Combine all of the above ingredients and refrigerate until ready for use.

Serves 6

Saturday Dinner

MENU
(for 6)

Steamed and Seared White Fish Fillets
Turnip Custard
Rice and Fresh Corn
Tea Sherbet
Ginger Cookies
Wine
Coffee

Tea sherbet with delicate ginger cookies.

Left: *The combination of flavors and colors in this Oriental-inspired dinner is wonderful.*

Saturday Dinner

D o the sherbet in the afternoon and store in the freezer. Do the Turnip Custard and set aside; before guests arrive, reheat and then unmold onto a serving plate. Make the cookies anytime.

When the corn and rice are finished, turn on the fish steamer. You will then have about 15 minutes to go, if everything else is ready.

Steamed and Seared White Fish Fillets

This method of cooking gives fish a marvelous flavor.

- 3 pounds flounder fillets
- ½ cup peanut oil
- 3 bunches green onion with some top, chopped in rings
- 2 or more tablespoons soy sauce

Oil the surface of the poaching cradle of a long fish poacher and put a piece of foil in it, allowing the foil to extend over the sides so that you can get a hold on it. Grease this. Arrange the fillets in a layer, not thicker than 1½ inches. Make a long fish shape. Put in steamer over an inch of water. You can set the cradle on a couple of little custard cups or any other low heatproof objects that will support it. Steam for approximately 15 minutes, or until fish is done in the middle.

While this is cooking, start heating the oil and have the serving platter, onions, and soy sauce ready. When the fish is done, slide it off the steamer tray onto the serving platter. You are more likely to be able to keep the fish intact if you slide it onto the dish with the foil underneath and then slide foil out. Turn up heat under oil; it must be smoking. If fish gets a little disarranged, pat back into shape. Drain off any water which might have accumulated in the platter. Sprinkle fish very generously with soy sauce (at least 2 tablespoons) and onions. Pour the smoking oil over the length of the fish and serve immediately with extra soy

sauce on the side. To serve, cut fish into narrow chunks.

Serves 6

Turnip Custard

Turnips prepared this way are mild and have a subtle flavor that is perfect with fish.

- 12 ounces white turnips (weigh after peeling)
- 1 3-ounce white potato (weigh after peeling)
- 3 tablespoons butter
- 2 large eggs
- ½ cup milk
- 3 tablespoons evaporated skimmed milk
- ½ teaspoon nutmeg
- ½ teaspoon salt, or to taste

Chopped parsley

Put kettle of water on to boil. Butter a 9-inch cake pan and set the oven rack in the middle position. Preheat to 375 degrees.

Boil the turnips until very tender, about 30 minutes. If they are large, cut into several pieces. Cut the potato into pieces and boil it until tender. Do this separately. In a food processor with a metal blade, process the turnips and butter until puréed, about 10 seconds. You may have to stop and scrape down the sides of the bowl. Add the remaining ingredients, except the potato, and process for 30 seconds. Push the potato through a fine sieve, add to the mixture. Adjust seasoning if necessary.

Pour the mixture into the cake pan and set it into a larger ovenproof pan. Surround with boiling water to come up ½ inch. Put in the oven and cook for 30 minutes, until the custard sets. Remove from water bath and let rest. If you have trouble getting the pan out of the bath, you can remove the hot water with a bulb baster. When ready to serve, run a knife around the edge and invert onto a platter. Decorate with chopped parsley.

Note: This custard can be prepared ahead and set aside, unmolded. Reheat by putting in water bath and simmering for 30 minutes on top of stove. When unmolding it, if parts should stick, carefully remove them with a spatula and mold the parts together with your hands. You will hardly be able to see the seams, and the parsley garnish will also help hide any imperfections.

Serves 6

Rice and Fresh Corn

These two grains are a natural combination and lend texture to this meal.

1¼	cups long-grain rice
3	to 4 cups chicken stock
8	large ears of corn
2	to 3 tablespoons milk
2	tablespoons (¼ stick) unsalted butter
	Salt to taste
	Dash of pepper

Cover the rice with chicken stock in a saucepan, then add another 2 cups. Bring to a boil, cook for 10 minutes, then test for doneness. Drain and keep warm.

Cut and scrape corn from cobs and put in a large skillet. Add milk. Bring to a simmer, covered, and let simmer for 1 minute. Mix with rice, butter, salt, and pepper. Correct seasoning and serve.

Note: This dish can be prepared at the last minute because the corn cooks such a short time. Do the rice, and just before you want to serve, start simmering the corn. It will hold a few minutes, covered, before you mix it with the rice.

Serves 6

Tea Sherbet

You must use a good, strong, black tea for this to give the sherbet enough flavor.

1	cup boiling water
2	tablespoons black tea leaves
1½	cups sugar
1	cup cold water
	Grated rind and juice of 1 lime
	Grated rind and juice of 1 orange
¼	cup dark rum
2	egg whites

Pour boiling water over the tea leaves and let sit for 10 minutes. Strain and set aside to cool.

Combine the sugar and cold water with the lime and orange rind. Bring to a boil and boil over moderate-high heat for 5 minutes. Remove from the heat and add the fruit juices, rum, and tea. Chill.

Beat the egg whites until they stand in stiff peaks, and fold into the tea mixture. Transfer to an automatic ice cream freezer. Store in the freezer until ready to serve.

Serves 6

Ginger Cookies

This recipe comes from the Loaves & Fishes store in Sagaponac, New York. The cookies are delicate and will get soggy, so it is best to use them the day they are made.

1	cup (2 sticks) unsalted butter
1	cup brown sugar, tightly packed
1	egg, beaten
1	cup flour
1	teaspoon baking powder
2	tablespoons fresh ginger, peeled and grated

Preheat the oven to 350 degrees. Butter a cookie sheet.

Cream butter and sugar. Beat in the egg. Sift the flour and baking powder together and stir into the egg mixture. Add the grated ginger.

Drop small balls of dough, the size of grapes, from a teaspoon onto a buttered cookie sheet. Bake for 6 to 8 minutes, or until the edges begin to brown. Watch carefully. Remove to a rack to cool.

Note: The most important thing to be aware of here is the consistency of the dough, which must be right or the cookies will flatten out too much. The first time you make these, you might test one or two on a small pan before doing the whole batch. The cooking time is so brief, it is worth the precaution. These cookies are supposed to be very thin, but if the dough is too runny the cookie will not hold its shape. Add a sprinkling of flour to correct the consistency if necessary.

Makes approximately 2 dozen cookies

Sunday Lunch

Sunday lunch served under a billowing canopy on the deck at my house. The boiled beef left over from lunch on Saturday is sliced thin and served with lemon wedges and hot mustards, along with steamed leeks, strong vinaigrette dressing, and the leftover asparagus. Baked chili-tomato eggs in bread crumb cups add interest to the meal, along with spicy poached bananas for dessert.

Poached bananas.

159

Sunday Lunch

MENU

(for 6)

Sliced Boiled Brisket (leftover)
with Hot Mustards
Chili-Tomato Eggs in Bread Crumb Cups
Asparagus (leftover)
Strong Vinaigrette (leftover)
Leeks
Poached Bananas
Wine
Iced Tea or Coffee

The only things you have to contend with here are the eggs and a dessert, and if poaching bananas is too tedious, forget about them and serve cookies and sherbet. By this point in the weekend you should be able to con someone into setting the table.

Leftovers

Bring the asparagus, vinaigrette, and brisket to room temperature. Slice the brisket very thin and serve with hot mustards.

Chili-Tomato Eggs in Bread Crumb Cups

These make a very pretty presentation. Any left over are good to take to the beach or on a picnic. They take a little doing, but since you don't have much else to worry with, give them a try. The recipe is in two parts and the cups can be done ahead of time.

Bread Crumb Cups
9   slices white bread, cut into quarters
3/4 cup (1 1/2 sticks) unsalted butter
1   teaspoon salt
1/2 teaspoon pepper
2   egg whites

Filling
6   large eggs
1/2 teaspoon salt
4   tablespoons safflower oil
1   cup seeded, peeled, and chopped tomatoes
3   tablespoons chopped white onion
3   tablespoons chopped sweet red pepper
1   small hot Mexican pepper, finely chopped
1   chili pepper, finely chopped

Preheat oven to 375 degrees. Grease six 3 1/2-inch muffin-tin cups. Cut a circle of waxed paper the size of the bottom of each cup. Put in cups and grease them.

Chop bread coarsely in a food processor, then bake on a cookie sheet for 10 minutes. Allow to cool. Put crumbs, butter, salt, and pepper into processor with a metal blade. Process briefly until mixture is crumbly but not pasty.

Beat egg whites until foamy and stir into crumb mixture. Divide among the cups and press against sides and bottom to form a shell. Bake approximately 15 minutes. Butter will foam up but will subside after it cools. This preparation may be done a day before and kept covered in the refrigerator (in the pan). Heat in the oven for 3 minutes before using.

To make filling, mix eggs lightly with salt and set aside. Put oil in skillet over high heat, add the tomatoes, onion, and peppers, and fry for about 2 minutes, stirring all the while (a bit longer if the tomatoes are giving off a lot of juice). Reduce heat and stir in eggs. Cook quickly until whites just begin to turn. Remove from heat and spoon into the prepared crumb cups. Bake 15 to 20 minutes. Timing will depend on how well done you want your eggs. They are practically cooked when you put them in the oven. Allow to cool just a few minutes before serving. Carefully loosen sides and lift out. Peel the waxed paper off carefully.

Makes 6 servings

Leeks

You don't have to do these if you have enough asparagus left over.

12   medium to small leeks, carefully washed and trimmed
Chicken stock

Cut the root off the leeks and cut the tops down practically to the white. Stand on root end and slice halfway down length of stem with a sharp knife. This will make it easier for the water to reach any sand that may be between the leaves. Soak in water for about ½ hour. Inspect carefully.

Cover with chicken stock and simmer until very tender, about 15 to 20 minutes. Let cool in the stock.

Note: Save any leftover leek–chicken stock to make Escarole Soup (page 77).

Poached Bananas

Peaches or pears that have been peeled and halved can be poached in this delicious spicy liquid too. Just make sure that it covers the fruit completely.

1   cup dark rum
1   cup water
12   tablespoons dark brown sugar
1   stick cinnamon
Peel of ¼ orange, cut into ½-inch strips
6   small, firm, ripe bananas, peeled
4   tablespoons heavy cream

Ice cream (optional)

Put rum, water, sugar, cinnamon stick, and orange peel in a saucepan just large enough to hold the bananas comfortably. Bring to a simmer, covered. Simmer 5 minutes before adding the fruit. These can be cooked whole if they are small enough, or halved lengthwise. Simmer until soft, about 5 minutes more. Remove carefully.

Boil liquid quickly to reduce by half to form a syrupy sauce. Stir in cream. Mix well and pour over the bananas. This can be served as is or with ice cream.

Serves 6

Assorted sausages ready for the grill.

Grated carrots dressed with hot walnut oil vinaigrette.

Sunday Dinner

A barbecue on Sunday is the perfect festive way to cap off a long weekend. The deck at my house is by the water, and the light is especially beautiful there late in the day. I sometimes try to time meals so that they can be eaten just as the afternoon light has faded and is turning magically into evening.

Baked lima beans and pears.

Grated pecan spongecake with bourbon whipped cream.

Fried hot water bread with green onion filling.

Sunday Dinner

MENU

(for 8)

Assorted Grilled Sausages with Mustard
Baked Lima Beans and Pears
Grated Carrots with Hot Walnut Oil
Vinaigrette
Fried Hot Water Bread
Grated Pecan Spongecake
Wine
Coffee

The bean and pear dish in this menu must cook for at least 8 hours (and for up to 12), so it should be put on in the morning. You have to check it only once or twice during the day to make sure that your oven is maintaining the low temperature required.

The Grated Carrots with Hot Walnut Oil Vinaigrette and the Fried Hot Water Bread are not really meant to be eaten alone but to enhance the other elements of the meal. The carrot mixture is more like a condiment than a vegetable, and the bread, which resembles pizza dough, is a perfect vehicle for the spicy sausage.

Because the bread cooks so fast and should be served hot, it can be done when the sausages finish and have been left to stay warm by the fire. The dough could be made hours before. The dessert would have been made in the afternoon.

Assorted Grilled Sausages with Mustard

What you want here is variety: hot, mild, and maybe a novelty sausage or some sort of wurst. It is best to ask the butcher who sells them to you about the cooking time and method, as some need preboiling before they are put on the grill. Luckily, sausages hold very well once they are cooked, so you don't have to worry about one variety finishing before another. If you are serving 3 different kinds, allow 1 of each per guest.

Serve with several varieties of mustard.

Baked Lima Beans and Pears

Presoaked and cooked dried limas can also be used in this recipe, but I find it much easier to use frozen ones.

- 6 cups frozen lima beans (about 3½ 10-ounce packages)
- 6 large ripe pears, cored, peeled, and sliced
- ¼ cup light molasses
- ¼ cup brown sugar
- ¼ cup finely chopped onion
- 1 cup chicken broth
- 1 teaspoon salt
- Pepper to taste

Preheat oven to 180 to 200 degrees.

Combine all ingredients in a heavy casserole with a tight-fitting lid and bake, covered, for 8 hours or longer. If there is excess moisture in the crock at the end of the cooking time you can continue to bake them with the top ajar to evaporate part of it. Personally, it doesn't matter to me if they are a bit liquid. They can wait for hours in the turned-off oven after they are done.

Serves 8

Grated Carrots with Hot Walnut Oil Vinaigrette

Since this is essentially a condiment, I allow about ½ cup grated carrots per person.

4 cups coarsely grated carrots

Vinaigrette Dressing
3 tablespoons walnut oil
2 tablespoons safflower oil
2 tablespoons red wine vinegar
1 teaspoon Dijon mustard
1 teaspoon salt, or to taste
Dash of pepper

Put the carrots in the bowl in which they will be served. Whisk together the other ingredients and put into a small saucepan. When ready to serve, heat the vinaigrette and toss with the carrots.

Makes 4 cups

Fried Hot Water Bread

This dough can be prepared ahead and then refrigerated, to be used when you are ready to cook. I have left it at this point for up to 5 hours.

10 ounces flour
1 teaspoon salt
1 cup boiling water
1 cup chopped green onion, including some top
Safflower oil

Put flour and salt in a food processor fitted with a steel blade. Turn the machine on and pour the boiling water in through the top in a continuous stream. Continue processing for 45 seconds. Dough will be shiny and elastic. Put finished dough in a tightly fitting plastic bag or plastic wrap and let rest at room temperature for 30 minutes.

Meanwhile, sauté the green onions in a bit of oil until they are wilted.

When the dough has rested, turn it out onto a floured surface and roll out with a floured rolling pin to a rectangle approximately 14 × 16 inches.

Spoon the wilted green onion evenly over the dough and roll jelly roll fashion, from the short side. Cut into 12 rounds. Put each between two sheets of lightly floured waxed paper and press down with the palm of your hand until it makes a flat circle. You can refrigerate it at this point.

To cook, put an inch of safflower oil in a large heavy skillet and fry each cake until golden brown. Turn once. This goes very quickly, so watch them carefully.

Makes 1 dozen cakes

Grated Pecan Spongecake

This cake was very popular with our family when I was growing up. We had lots of pecans around so they were always used, but I don't see why other nuts wouldn't work equally well.

1½ cups granulated sugar
6 large eggs, separated
3 tablespoons cake flour
1 teaspoon baking powder
3 cups grated pecans (measure after grating)
¼ teaspoon cream of tartar

½ cup heavy cream, whipped, sweetened, and spiked with bourbon

Preheat oven to 375 degrees and lightly grease a tube pan.

Sift the sugar and combine it with the egg yolks. Beat until they are lemon yellow and set aside. Sift the cake flour, sprinkle it with baking powder, and sift once more. Mix with the chopped nuts.

Beat the egg whites until foamy. Sprinkle in the cream of tartar and continue to whip until they stand in stiff peaks. Heap the egg whites on the nut-flour mixture and gently fold them in, turning the mixture over and over. Do not stir or beat. When this is completed, it should be a bit lumpy. Carefully combine with the egg yolk–sugar mixture, using the same method. Pour and scrape into the tube pan.

Bake for approximately 30 minutes, or until a cake tester comes out clean. Turn upside down on a rack and allow to cool. Gently loosen sides and remove from pan.

Serve with sweetened whipped cream spiked with bourbon. Use a lot of bourbon.

Makes one 9-inch tube cake

Poached chicken breasts with lemon yogurt sauce; low-calorie cottage cheese mixed with chives, radishes, sweet red peppers, toasted pecans; and homemade melba toast.

Ice tea, the classic of summer.

Low-calorie cottage cheese mixed with fresh pineapple, strawberry sauce made with fresh puréed strawberries and lemon juice, melon balls, and homemade melba toast.

Monday Diet Lunches

Monday Diet Lunches

After a long weekend of eating and a bit of overindulging, I find guests are often happy to have a diet lunch before leaving. It seems to square their consciences—and sometimes mine. These lunches are very tasty in and of themselves, but of equal importance is the fact that they *look* like diet lunches. That is, they are made up of foods literally recognized as being low in calories and often associated with dieting. This is important psychologically, I think. Then when your guests find it all tastes good too, well!

I have made two menus for you to choose from, neither one of which is difficult. I like them both equally well. For the first menu, I shred the pineapple rather fine, stir it in with the cottage cheese, and refrigerate it. Any melons may be used. They don't necessarily have to be balled; they just make a nicer presentation that way. The strawberry sauce is just puréed strawberries with a bit of lemon juice (and grated rind if you like) and artificial sweetener if the berries are too tart (go easy on the sweetener). If you have never made melba toast, once you do you will never buy the commercial kind. Use any very thin bread (thinner than regular sandwich bread) cut in half and arranged on a cookie sheet. Allow to sit in a 200-degree oven for several hours to dry out and become golden.

The second menu requires you to poach chicken breasts, but this only takes 10 minutes or so, depending on how big they are. Bring chicken stock to a simmer or use the stock in which you cooked leeks and drop the boned and halved breasts in. Simmer until they are white and elastic to the touch. You can peep inside one if you are not sure. Allow to cool in the stock. Mix lemon juice and grated rind with low-fat yogurt (and some dill if you like). Serve on the side. The chives, radishes, sweet peppers, and pecans are tossed lightly in the cottage cheese just before serving. Make melba toast as above.

MENU

*Low-Calorie Cottage Cheese Mixed with
Fresh Pineapple*
Two Kinds of Melon Balls
Strawberry Sauce
Freshly Made Melba Toast
Iced Tea

MENU

*Poached Chicken Breasts with
Lemon Yogurt Sauce*
*Low-Calorie Cottage Cheese Mixed with
Chives, Radishes, Sweet Red Peppers,
and Toasted Pecans*
Freshly Made Melba Toast
Iced Tea

Acknowledgments

With love and thanks to my dear old friend Amy Gross, who not only wrote the introduction for this book but was expert at keeping such a reluctant stone as I am rolling. And thanks to another old friend and gentle pressure expert, Gloria Safier, my agent, who got me to Clarkson Potter. To Carol Southern, a kindred spirit who has the courage to trust her instincts, and to Sarah Wright, who seemed to like the idea of the book from the beginning and said so. To Carolyn Hart, my editor, who managed to smile away all my insecurities and keep me on the track with that quality of effortlessness that I find so appealing. And to all the other people at Clarkson Potter who have been so generous with their time and help (with special thanks to Gael Dillon for burning the midnight oil).

To Joshua Greene, the talented young photographer who made so beautifully visual what was only an idea in my head. Thanks to Linda too.

To Rochelle Udell, who designed this book with an ease and grace that was breathtaking and yet always had time to explain and make sure we were in agreement. My thanks to Doug too.

To Eddie Benham, my assistant on this project, who has got to be one of the best-natured and hardest-working souls around. Thanks pal.

To Carole Bannett, who has worked with me for almost ten years and who managed, often at the expense of her own comfort, to keep the world at bay so I could finish on schedule (another smiling pressure expert now that I think of it.)

To Florence Fink, who is always available to help in any way she can, and to Barbara Gray. To Iris, who kept trying to get the picture right, and to Lee Klein and Marshall Young for giving me a quiet and beautiful place to work. To Claude Langwith, who tested recipes nonstop for an entire weekend.

To my aunt, Freddie Bailey, a natural and giving cook, for years of love and support and recipes, and to her daughter, my sweet cousin, Freddie Gee. And to my aunt, Cora Bailey, another natural cook, who sent recipes and helpful suggestions.

To the friends and acquaintances, old and new, who so generously lent their houses and possessions. My appreciation to Ward Bennett, Mr. and Mrs. Arnold Segal, Bob Bear, Tim Romonella, Tom Fallon, Diane Fisher, Barbara Bach, and Joe Eula. To Neal Koppel, who took us for a sail and picture-taking session, and to Anne Aspinal of the Topping Riding Club, who arranged for us to photograph her young riders. And to Donald Spellman, thanks for the jeep.

To three very special friends, who not only graciously gave me the use of their houses and gardens (and kitchens) but always something more: to Geraldine Stutz, unfailingly filled with enthusiasm and encouragement, my love and thanks. To Peter Schub for his accurate advice and for getting me together with Rochelle Udell. And to Nora Ephron for being the kind of good friend she is.

To my buddy, Christopher Idone, who is the most stylish person in the food business. To David Luck, always willing to help. To Liz Smith for picking raspberries. To Bob McIntosh, who gave me his old typewriter and his ear. And to Mildred, Judy, Lynn, Gael, Bernie, Tony, Larry, Fred, and Margo.

Thanks to Dorothy, Kevin, Claire, and all the gang at Dean & DeLuca for making it easier, and to Peachie Halsey of the Green Thumb, who is just what her name sounds like, and to her crew.

To the proprietors of the beautiful little shops in and around my country hometown, Bridgehampton, New York, for their generosity. Among them is Richard Camp, one of the first people to collect and value those affordable "almost antiques" that are so popular today. Many things in the photographs are from him.

To Susan Costner of C. & W. Mercantile, whose meticulously selected merchandise can be seen in the "At the Beach" picture. Thanks to Edith Lewis of House of Charm Antiques for the big white wicker chairs in the "Under the Pines" picture. And to Don Zornow, owner of The American Wing, thanks for the chairs and all sorts of interesting stuff sprinkled in pictures throughout the book.

To my colleague at Henri Bendel Inc., Frank McIntosh, my appreciation for the table setting that appears in the "Under the Pines" picture. To Porcelaine d'Auteuil for the elegant tureens in the gumbo picture.

Last, but certainly not least, to Claudia Shwide and Barbara Eigen, two wonderful potters with whom I have worked for years, thanks for being so generous.

Index

About the Author

Lee Bailey is a designer whose work has been
featured in the design and home furnishings
sections of most major magazines in the country,
including *House & Garden, House Beautiful, Vogue,*
and the *New York Times Magazine.* Mr. Bailey
now markets his work through his own shop at
Bendel's in New York.

 Born in Louisiana, Mr. Bailey has taught design
at the Parsons School of Design and Tulane
University. He lives in New York City and on
eastern Long Island. This is his first book.